Why Suffer?

PERIODS AND THEIR PROBLEMS

LYNDA BIRKE
Research Fellow in Biology at The Open University
&
KATY GARDNER *GP*

Acknowledgements

We are grateful to Dr Brush, at St Thomas's Hospital in London, for a useful discussion on possible causes of premenstrual tension. He and his colleagues have spent much time researching into premenstrual tension, and until recently ran a clinic to help women with premenstrual problems.

We are also very grateful to Sandy Best, who did some of the graphics, and to women of the Brighton Women and Science Group for helpful ideas and comments on the manuscript.

We are indebted to the History and Social Studies of Science Department of the University of Sussex, which provided Lynda Birke with facilities while this book was being written.

We are also indebted to the various women who have helped us to gain a better understanding of the problems they face associated with menstruation – women in feminist health groups, women to whom we have spoken at various times and places about PMT, as well as all the women who have written to us since the publication of the first edition.

First published in Great Britain by VIRAGO PRESS Limited 1979
41 William IV Street, London WC2N 4DB
2nd edition 1982, reprinted 1984

British Library Cataloguing in Publication Data

Birke, Lynda
Why suffer?
1. Menstruation disorders
I. Title II. Gardner, Katy
618.1'72 RG161

ISBN 0-86068-284-6

Printed and bound in Great Britain by
Anchor Brendon Ltd, Tiptree, Essex

Contents

Preface to Second Edition

Since the first edition of *Why Suffer?* came out, we have heard from a large number of women suffering from period problems, particularly PMT. Many of them have told us of premenstrual symptoms which we did not mention in the book, such as food cravings, nightmares, feeling sexier than usual, an inability to string words together correctly. Many have written to thank us; they tried some of the things we suggest in the book, such as Vitamin B6, and found that they worked. We are really pleased to hear this, and hope that the second edition will help many more women.

We have been impressed by the wide range of experiences women have; some even report problems at the *end* of a period rather than before it starts. We have also been impressed – and pleased – to discover that many women have organised themselves into groups to deal with their problems. One group of women organised a discussion group in their factory after discovering that they were synchronising, and so were all having period problems at about the same time. They found that the discussions in the group helped them a lot. Perhaps the most cheering letter from a reader was from the woman who wrote telling us about her changed relationship with her doctor. She said: 'Thanks so much for giving me the courage and knowledge on the subject to be able to go and ask him in the first place. I think I still have some way to go towards full "recovery" but the whole experiment has brought a better understanding between my GP and myself and I'm sure it's also made him sit up and take notice of the needs of other affected women under his care.'

Preface

This book is intended primarily as a guide to dealing with problems associated with having periods. It also explains some basic biology of the menstrual cycle. We have tried to avoid using too many medical words which serve to mystify. Where we have used technical words, we have explained their meaning in the text, but we have also included a glossary at the beginning of the book. This explains simply all the technical words we have used.

Where we have advocated that particular problems are best dealt with by a doctor, we have not assumed that everyone has a male doctor. More and more women are entering medicine. Thus, whenever reference is made to doctors, we have used the abbreviated 's/he' : ie, she or he. On the whole, we have assumed that the majority of readers of this book will be women – although we would be delighted if men read it too, to enable them to understand better some of the problems women face.

GLOSSARY

Adrenals: The adrenals are small glands situated on top of the kidneys. They produce many different hormones, most of which are steroid hormones. Hormones from the adrenals influence mineral and carbohydrate balance (ie. the rate at which you burn up sugars), among other things.
Aldactone: This is the name of a specific drug (proper name, spironolactone) which inhibits the action of aldosterone, a hormone from the adrenals.
Aldosterone: This is a steroid hormone secreted by the adrenal glands, and which is involved in mineral balance. Some doctors believe it to be involved in premenstrual tension.
Amenorrhoea: This means cessation of periods. The most usual cause is pregnancy, but periods can stop for a number of other reasons too (see page 59).

Androgens: These are hormones produced in large quantities by a man's testes, and in much smaller quantities by a woman's ovaries. They are also produced in small quantities by the adrenal glands of both women and men.
Anovulatory Cycles: This means a menstrual cycle in which ovulation does not occur, although the ovarian hormones have built up a lining of the womb which breaks down and bleeds at the usual time. Anovulatory cycles are quite common in young women before their cycles are fully established.
Bromocriptine: A drug given for premenstrual tension. It works by counteracting the hormone prolactin, which tends to retain fluids. Thus, bromocriptine is especially useful for problems with fluid retention and breast tenderness.
Carbohydrates: A particular constituent of food. Sugars of all kinds (eg. honey, ordinary sugar, treacle, milk, sugar and so on) and starches (eg. as found in flour and potatoes) are forms of carbohydrate. Carbohydrates have a high calorie value, and are important energy foods.
Cervix: The 'neck' of the womb, which projects downwards into the vagina. It can be seen as a doughnut shape when the vagina is opened with a speculum.
Clomiphene: This is the name of a drug given to stimulate ovulation, and thus to bring on menstruation. It works by stimulating oestrogen production from the ovaries, which in turn stimulates ovulation.
Congenital: Something inborn. This could either be as a result of inheritance, or as a result of a process of early development, while the child is still in the womb. It is nearly always used with reference to something going wrong during early development, as in 'congenital absence of ovaries'.
Consciousness-raising: A process of increasing one's awareness of one's social and political position through group discussion. It is specifically used in the Women's Liberation Movement to help women to understand their own situation and oppression as women.
Corpus Luteum: The scar, or yellow body, remaining in the ovary after the egg has been shed at ovulation. The corpus luteum is the chief source of the hormone progesterone.
Dilation & Curettage: Commonly called a D.& C. It is an operation under general anaesthesia in which the lining of the womb is scraped with an instrument called a curette, following slight dilation (opening) of the cervix to allow the curette to enter the womb.
Diuretics: Drugs which increase the volume of urine passed, by acting on the tubules of the kidney.
Dysmenorrhoea: Pain accompanying periods.
Endometriosis: A condition in which small pieces of the lining of the uterus come to lie elsewhere, such as in the abdominal cavity. It is

usually accompanied by severe pain.

Fallopian tubes: The tubes along which the egg is carried from the ovary to the uterus. Fertilisation occurs in the Fallopian tubes. Very rarely, the fertilised egg begins to grow in the tubes. This is called an *ectopic* pregnancy, and is a medical emergency, accompanied by severe abdominal pain.

Fibroids: Small lumps of tissue growing out from the wall of the womb. They can cause considerable pain, and may have to be removed surgically.

Flufenamic acid: A drug which might be given to relieve period pain. It works by counteracting the prostaglandins (see below).

Galactorrhoea: Excessive milk secretion from the breast. This can sometimes occur even when a woman has not recently had a baby (see pp. 63).

Gonadotrophins: Hormones secreted by the pituitary gland. They stimulate the ovaries (or the testes in a man) to secrete their own hormones, as well as stimulating them to release an egg when it is mature.

Graafian follicle: The name given to a mature ovum, surrounded by a bag of fluid within the ovary.

IUD (Intra-Uterine Device): Commonly known as the coil or the loop, a device inserted within the uterus for contraception.

Mefanimic acid: A specific drug known to help period pains. It works by counteracting prostaglandins in the uterus. It is marketed as 'Ponstan'.

Menorrhagia: Excessive blood loss at each period.

Minerals: Substances such as iron, calcium, magnesium, sodium, potassium. All of these are essential in the diet.

Mittelschmerz: Literally, it means 'middle pain'. It is a term referring to pain associated with ovulation, half-way between periods.

Norethisterone: A commonly used progestin. It is contained in many brands of the Pill.

Oestrogens: A group of steroid hormones secreted in large quantities by the ovaries, and to a lesser extent by the adrenals and a man's testes. They cause the development of secondary sexual characteristics, such as the growth of breasts, and are involved in the control of the menstrual cycle. The Pill usually contains a synthetic oestrogen.

Ovary: The structure (of which there are normally two) in the female which produces eggs and steroid hormones such as oestrogens. The ovaries are situated either side of the womb (uterus) between the hips.

Ovulation: The release of a ripe egg, or ovum, from the ovary. Ovulation is controlled by hormones (gonadotrophins) released by the pituitary.

Ovum: The egg which is released from the ovary at ovulation.
Pituitary: A small gland situated at the base of the brain, secreting many hormones, among which are those that stimulate the ovary.
'Ponstan': A specific drug known to help period pains. It works by counteracting prostaglandins in the uterus. Its chemical name is mefanimic acid.
Premenstrual syndrome: (or PMS). This means much the same thing as **premenstrual tension** – a complex set of changes which accompany the premenstrual time and which often cause distress to the women experiencing them.
Progesterone: A specific hormone secreted by the corpus luteum of the ovary (see above). It is an important hormone for the maintenance of early pregnancy. It has been suggested (see p.34) that a progesterone deficiency causes some of the problems of premenstrual tension.
Progestins: A group of hormones having similar effects on the body to natural progesterone. **Progestins** refers to all those hormones having similar effects, including progesterone itself.
Prolactin: The hormone secreted by the pituitary and which is involved in milk production. Some doctors also believe it to be involved in premenstrual tension (see p.35), as some anti-prolactin drugs can relieve premenstrual problems, such as bloating. It is also involved in some cases of amenorrhoea (see p.63).
Prostaglandins: Substances found within the body of the uterus itself, and which cause the uterus to contract more forcefully. Prostaglandins are important in the initiation of labour, and are sometimes used to induce labour. They may also be involved in period pain.
Pyridoxine: Vitamin B6. Some doctors believe it to be deficient in women on the Pill, and in women suffering from severe premenstrual tension. It can be given to women suffering especially from depression and bloating, and appears to relieve these symptoms of premenstrual tension quite effectively.
Steroids: Substances having a particular chemical structure. All the 'sex' hormones such as oestrogens, progestins and androgens are steroids.
Thyroid: A gland situated in the neck, and producing the hormone thyroxine. It was once thought to be involved in premenstrual tension, although few doctors now believe this.
Uterus: The medical name for the womb.
Vitamins: Substances essential for the body, normally obtained from our food. There are several different kinds of vitamin, and to stay healthy we need to have an adequate intake of all of them. The most important ones in the context of this book are the B vitamins, which are obtained largely from green vegetables, wheatgerm, wholemeal flour, and meat.

Introduction

This book is intended as a source of help and information for women who suffer with their periods. It can also be a source of information for anyone who wants to understand more about menstruation, and the problems which some women have with it. It is essentially a practical book, aiming to provide information about the possible ways to deal with certain period problems, such as premenstrual tension, period pain, or having irregular periods. Since we know that many women today are wary of taking drugs unless they are absolutely sure that they need them, we have emphasised answers which are basically self-help answers. But we have not forgotten that for many women these will not be sufficient, and we have therefore included in each chapter a section on treatments available through the doctor. In some cases, of course, self-help is not advisable – as in cases of sudden bleeding from the vagina – so we stress the importance of seeking medical advice in such cases.

We recognise that it must be an individual woman's choice, whether she would prefer to seek a doctor's help: only she knows how bad her menstruation makes her feel. We have tried to provide information about a variety of different solutions to the same problems, in order that women can make an *informed* choice between available alternatives. Too often, people attend the doctor and are given a prescription for something-or-other, and are told little or nothing either about their problem, or about the drug which they have been given.

In addition, unlike many other books giving information about the menstrual cycle, this one does *not* favour exclusively medical theories of menstrual problems such as premenstrual tension. We know that the menstrual cycle is still under-researched. But in addition to any research reported in medical journals, there are reports in psychology journals. These tend to indicate that menstruation is far more than simply a question of biology. We all experience it in particular ways which reflect, among other factors, the values of the society of which we are part. Women living in other societies throughout the world experience menstruation differently: many, for example, do not have 'premenstrual tension' at all, and others experience a quite different range of 'symptoms' of premenstrual tension from Western women.

WHAT IS PREMENSTRUAL TENSION?

The term premenstrual tension is used to refer to those bodily changes and mood swings which occur in some women just before a period is due: changes such as weight gain, spots, irritability, inability to concentrate and anxiety are all reported by women. These changes may be uncomfortable, and annoying, but we should emphasise that they hardly constitute a disease, as some doctors have implied. One thing is quite clear: whatever uncomfortable changes a woman may experience, she usually knows that they will disappear when her period arrives. Nevertheless, it is also clear that a few women experience bodily changes which are particularly distressing, and which may last for a fortnight. Serious problems can arise – a woman might become excessively irritable with her children (for which she may feel guilty afterwards), she may be unable to cope with her work, or she may spend days crying for no apparent reason. Life, in other words, becomes intolerable for a short while, both for the sufferer and for those people with whom she lives.

For most women, however, the problems are not so great. It is true that the majority of women experience some changes, either in their bodies, or in their moods, but relatively few find these incapacitating. The term premenstrual tension is applied to all women who experience these changes before a period, whether very mildly, or very severely. For the majority whose problems are not severe, it does not seem appropriate to us to refer to premenstrual tension as though it is a disease best treated by drugs. We prefer to call it an uncomfortable state of the body – which is, after all, temporary.

For the minority, however, whose symptoms are particularly severe, it may be more appropriate to think of premenstrual tension as a symptom of some kind of imbalance in the body which might be treated by drugs. Whether or not a woman wishes to try and deal with her problems herself, or whether she wishes to take drugs, must be her own decision.

Most of us prefer our lives to be fairly predictable. This is why premenstrual mood swings, or period pains, can so often be a nuisance: they tend to disrupt our lives and ruin our plans. In our grandmothers' days, women were told that such problems were part of being a woman, and they would have to 'grin and bear it'. Today, we still know far too little about menstruation and its problems: but we do know that there are a number of things that women can do to ease those problems. Women do not have to grin and bear it at all. It is ways of dealing with these problems which form the theme of this book.

1 The menstrual cycle

Every woman is aware of one obvious feature of her cycle: menstrual bleeding. But there are many ways in which the body changes during the course of one cycle. We may or may not notice other changes such as weight gain, breast tenderness, or a change in vaginal secretions. In this chapter, we are dealing mainly with physical changes occurring during the cycle, while we deal with changes in mood and behaviour in the following chapter.

The menstrual cycle is extremely complex, and poorly understood even by doctors. What is known is that various changes occur not only in the womb, but throughout the body. These are usually the result of changes in the quantity of the hormones secreted by the ovaries. A woman's sensitivity to smell, for example, is greatest about half-way between periods, and least around the time of menstruation. This change is influenced by the hormone *oestrogen.*

The major changes which accompany the menstrual cycle are listed in Table 1 (p. 8), although we may not have managed to include every possible change. If you experience cyclic changes which are not explained in this book, and which you want to know more about, you should ask your doctor to explain them to you. Similarly, if you feel that something is wrong with your cycle, you should consult your doctor and ask her/him to explain to you what is wrong. If you do not get an adequate explanation, or get one which you do not understand, don't be too embarrassed to ask for a fuller explanation. An answer is not much good if you cannot understand it. Too many women know too little about how their bodies work, and are often further mystified by statements made by doctors.

Some parts of this chapter deal with particularly complex subjects, such as the hormonal changes of the menstrual cycle. You will need to read the entire chapter if you are to understand the changes of the cycle, but do not be put off if there is one section which you do not fully understand. The biology of menstruation *is* very complex. We have included it in this book as it may help readers to understand better what the bodily changes involve. Understanding this chapter is useful, but it is not essential.

TABLE 1: SOME BODILY CHANGES OCCURRING DURING THE MENSTRUAL CYCLE

1 *Changes around the time of menstruation*

Bodily movements increase (such as small limb-movements) and decrease after menstruation
Excretion of vitamin A is at its lowest
Blood sugar (when you are hungry) is higher at menstruation
Urine output increases

2 *Changes around the time of ovulation*

Temperature (taken before getting up in the morning) goes up by about one degree
Slight increase in weight
Amount of cholesterol in blood goes down
Blood calcium levels high
Excretion of vitamin C at its lowest
Maximum sensitivity to smells
Bodily movements increase again, and decrease after ovulation

3 *Between ovulation and menstruation*

Slight increase in pulse rate
Less potassium and sodium lost in urine
Fewer active sweat glands

4 *Premenstrually*

Weight increase
Blood calcium levels low
Urine output decreases
Thyroid gland (in the neck) enlarges very slightly
Greater chance of getting some diseases (e.g. 'flu, typhoid, cold sores, boils, colds, conjunctivitis).

HORMONE CHANGES

The changes central to the menstrual cycle involve hormones secreted by the ovaries. The story of the hormones involved in the control of the cycle is a particularly complicated one, which we will only sketch out here. Hormones are substances secreted directly into the blood-stream, usually from specific organs such as the thyroid gland (which is situated in the neck), the adrenals (situated above the kidneys), or the ovaries (in the pelvic region). It was once thought that hormones are made and secreted only by these specific organs, the endocrine glands. However, it is now known that there are many exceptions to this, such as the hormones called the prostaglandins (see Glossary), which are produced all over the body.

Hormones are carried in the blood, and so can reach all parts of the body. We can, however, usually specify a 'target organ': that is, an organ of the body which is particularly sensitive to that hormone. For example, the ovaries produce hormones called *oestrogens,* to which the uterus (womb), vagina and breasts are especially sensitive.

The ovaries produce at least three different kinds of hormones. The most important are *oestrogens* and *progestins,* which are involved in the control of the menstrual cycle. The ovaries also produce small quantities of *androgens,* which are sometimes called 'male' hormones because men produce them in large quantities. All these hormones belong to a group of hormones called the steroids (the name describes the chemical structure). Steroids are principally produced from three sources: a woman's ovaries, a man's testes, and everyone's adrenal glands. Each of these glands – ovaries, testes, and adrenals – produce all three hormones, but in differing amounts. Thus, what differentiates female from male is the relative quantities of each kind of sex hormone produced: females produce more oestrogens and progestins, while males produce more androgens. There is no hormone which is exclusive to one sex or the other.

The amount of hormones in a woman's bloodstream varies considerably with the menstrual cycle, as shown in Figure 1. The diagram shows the changes in hormone levels at each stage of the cycle, and also illustrates the changes occurring in the womb, and within the ovaries. This diagram, of course, assumes that the cycle-length is twenty-eight days exactly. Twenty-eight days is the average cycle-length of all women, although most women do not have a cycle-length of exactly four weeks. Perfectly healthy women may have a gap between periods of as little as two weeks or as much as ten weeks, while others may not have regular cycles at all. However, for the sake of simplicity, twenty-eight days is usually taken as the average cycle length.

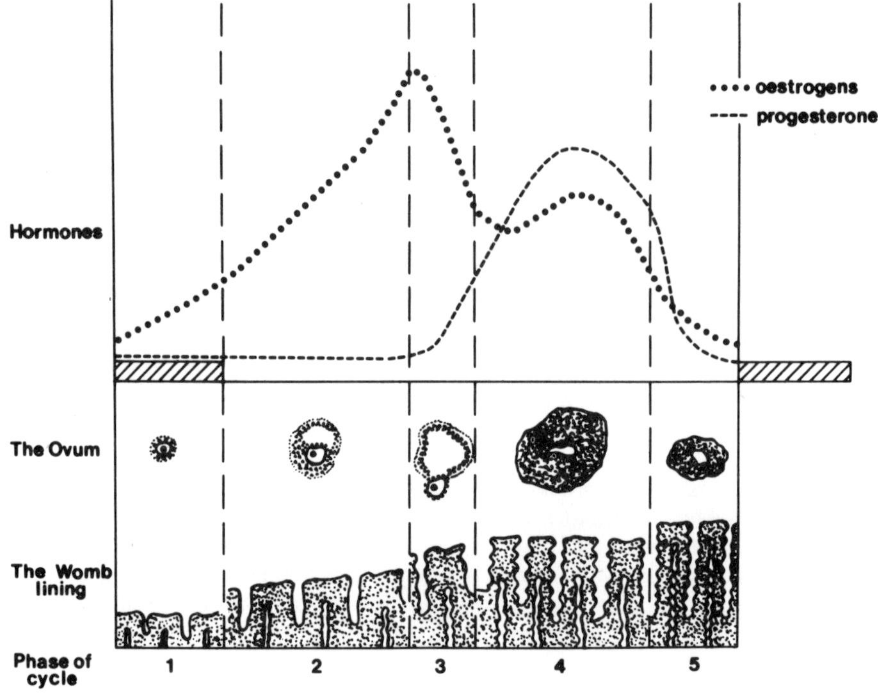

Figure 1. The Menstrual Cycle

This diagram shows the changes in the amounts of hormones produced by the ovaries during the menstrual cycle, and also shows the changes occurring in the ovum (egg), and in the womb lining. The hatched bar represents the time of bleeding. The cycle is divided up, roughly, into five phases, which are described in the text. During phase one (menstruation), the ovaries are producing quite low levels of hormones (see upper graph). At this time the egg is small, and the womb lining is thin. During phase two, the oestrogen levels increase, which makes the womb lining thicker. At the same time, the egg is maturing. Phase three is ovulation – when the egg is shed from the ovary. In phase four, the ovary produces both kinds of hormones, and the womb-lining becomes thicker still. The egg has left a scar (the corpus luteum) behind in the ovary. Phase five is the premenstrual phase: quantities of hormones are decreasing, and the corpus luteum is becoming smaller and eventually fades away. Then menstrual bleeding (phase one) starts again.

In the diagram, we have divided the cycle up, roughly, into five phases. The *first phase* is menstruation itself, during which the womb sheds its lining if the woman is not pregnant. (If pregnancy occurs, the lining nourishes and protects the developing foetus.) Both oestrogen and progestin levels are low during this phase.

The *second phase* lasts from the end of menstruation until just before ovulation, when the egg (ovum) is shed from the ovary. In a woman with a cycle-length of about 28 days, the egg is shed about 14 days after the start of the last period. During this second phase, the ovaries produce more and more oestrogen, until the oestrogen levels reach a maximum just before ovulation (see Figure 1). There is still very little progestin being produced, however. The high levels of oestrogen during this phase help to stimulate the release of the egg from the ovary.

The *third phase* involves ovulation itself, which, as the diagram shows, is accompanied by falling levels of oestrogen. At the time of ovulation, some women experience a sharp pain in their lower abdomen, around the ovaries and Fallopian tubes as the egg is shed: some also find that they bleed a little. This pain at ovulation is called 'mittelschmerz' which means, literally, 'middle pain', as it occurs halfway between periods. Pain at ovulation seems to accompany the release of the egg from the ovary. Only one ovum is normally shed each month, from one or the other ovary, so the pain will probably not always be on the same side. These pains are not usually as severe as period pains, and do not last very long, usually only a few hours.

Ovulation is the time of greatest fertility, so that women who wish to conceive should time their intercourse to coincide with their ovulation if possible. Ovulation is midway between periods in women who menstruate fairly regularly every 28 days. In those women who do not have such regular periods, ovulation tends to occur about 14 days before the next period. Thus, if you are a woman who menstruates approximately every 6 weeks, instead of every 4 (ie. every 42 days or so) then your most fertile time will probably be about 4 weeks after the start of your last period, and 2 weeks before the next period is due. If you are irregular, however, and you wish to conceive (or avoid conceiving), then it is best to determine the time at which you ovulate. This can be done by taking your temperature first thing in the morning before you get up every day, as ovulation is accompanied by a slight rise in body temperature (about a degree or so). We discuss other methods of determining the time of ovulation later in this chapter, in the section on changes in the vagina.

The *fourth phase* lasts from ovulation until the premenstrual period, that is from about day 14 to about day 24 in regular cycles. After the mature egg has left the ovary, it leaves behind a structure called the *corpus luteum* (which means 'yellow body', describing its appearance under the microscope). This structure secretes *progestins* into the bloodstream. Doctors call this phase the luteal phase. Both oestrogens and progestins are secreted during this phase, and begin to fall again just before menstruation starts.

The *fifth phase* is the premenstrual phase, a few days before the next period, during which the hormone levels fall again. It is during this phase that some women experience changes which they find unpleasant.

All of these complicated events are controlled by the *pituitary gland* situated at the base of the brain, which in turn secretes its own hormones. These latter hormones include the *gonadotrophins,* which stimulate the ovaries (or the testes in men). Gonadotrophins are responsible for stimulating the developing egg to mature, for bringing about ovulation of the mature egg, and for stimulating the ovaries to produce their own hormones.

WHAT HAPPENS TO THE OVARIES DURING THE CYCLE?

At the beginning of each cycle, the stimulation from the pituitary gland starts again, and a few eggs begin to mature. After about the sixth day, however, nearly all of these fade away, leaving only one to continue to grow to maturity. No one really knows how this one egg is singled out for development while all the others fade. All we know is that it is nearly always only one egg which matures. The only exceptions to this are (a) occasionally, two eggs are released at ovulation, and, if fertilisation occurs, non-identical twins result. Identical twins result if only one egg is matured which splits into two after fertilisation. (b) more than one egg might be released if a woman has been treated with the so-called 'fertility drug'. This is quite rare, but it is more likely than it is in women who have not received a drug. 'Fertility drugs' are discussed later in this book, as they are also sometimes given to women whose periods have for some reason stopped.

When the egg is fully mature, it is surrounded by a layer of cells inside a bag of fluid. At this stage it is called the *Graafian follicle.* Once it is mature, a signal from the pituitary gland causes it to break out of this fluid sac. It then enters the Fallopian tube, whose end is very close to the ovary, and is pushed along the tube by the action of tiny hairs. If fertilisation takes place, it normally does so in the Fallopian tube. The egg leaves behind it the structure known as the corpus luteum, which eventually fades away just before the next period is due. If a woman is pregnant, however, this structure persists for a while, and produces the hormones which are essential to pregnancy (the progestins) until the placenta has grown big enough to produce hormones instead. Without these hormones, the pregnancy will fail, and women producing too little of these hormones frequently miscarry. As the corpus luteum fades away, another egg begins to mature in the ovary.

When she is born, a woman carries all the eggs she will ever need – about 5 million of them. At about the time of her birth, each of these tiny eggs undergoes a special division, after which many perish, leaving about 500,000 to remain in waiting until she is an adult. Since only about 500 of these will ever fully mature (during approximately 40 years of having periods), that means that another 499,500 will perish. This seems like enormous wastage, but it probably represents nature's way of ensuring that faulty eggs do not mature. There may be a very small number of faulty eggs left after all this, but even if these become fertilised, very few indeed grow into babies. The majority of faulty eggs which are fertilised result in miscarriage.

WHAT HAPPENS TO THE UTERUS DURING THE CYCLE?

We have seen that hormones are produced by the ovary, and that these hormones fluctuate during the course of a cycle. The ovary itself changes with the monthly cycle, maturing and releasing an egg. If fertilised, that egg will normally end up growing in the uterus, or womb, which, in turn is prepared to receive it. Very rarely, the fertilised egg begins to grow in the Fallopian tubes. If it does, it causes acute pain, and has to be removed surgically. This is called an ectopic pregnancy.

At the end of menstruation, all but the deepest layers of the uterine wall have broken away and been shed, along with menstrual blood as a period. During phase two, oestrogens from the ovary cause the lining of the uterus to build up, and to thicken, ready to receive a fertilised egg if there is one. After ovulation, the ovary is secreting both types of hormone: the effect of the two together is to make the glands of the uterine lining more thickly folded. It is in this state that a fertilised egg can grow in the uterus.

If there is no fertilisation, then the ovary ceases to secrete large quantities of hormones about 14 days after the egg was released. This produces a decline in hormone levels (see Figure 1), which in turn causes the lining of the womb to break down. The bleeding of menstruation is due to the breakdown of the tiny arteries which form part of the womb's lining.

The human uterus builds up a layer of many of these tiny blood-vessels, so that we bleed as the lining breaks down. This is not the case in most other mammals, as their wombs do not build up many blood-vessels. Other mammals, such as dogs, cats, horses, sometimes bleed when they are on heat. This is the time when they ovulate, and so is equivalent to half-way between our periods: but their bleeding is not equivalent to our menstruation.

Many women feel that they have very heavy periods, and that they are losing enormous quantities of blood. This is not really true: the average amount of blood lost in each period is only about 30 to 40 millilitres – about two eggcupsful. Figure 2 shows the proportion of women losing different amounts of blood at each period. Most of us, as you will see, lose about 30-40 mls, but some lose less than 10 mls, and some more than 90 mls. It appears more because the uterine lining is shed as well.

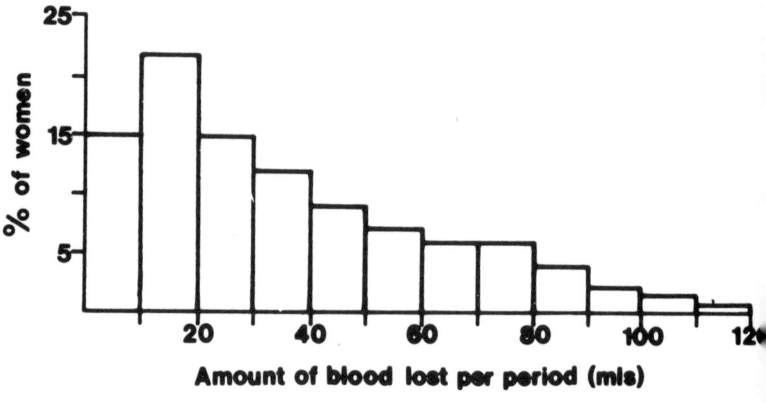

Figure 2. Diagram to show the amount of blood lost in a period

This bar chart shows the amount of blood lost by different women in each period. On the left hand side is the percentage of women losing particular quantities of blood: the quantities of blood are along the bottom. This means that 15 out of every 100 women lose less than 10 millilitres (ml) of blood in one period (less than an eggcupful): 22 out of 100 lose between 10 and 20 millilitres (ml) and so on. The *average* blood loss is between 30 and 40 millilitres, although clearly some women lose much less, and some much more. Very rarely, a woman might lose more than 120 millilitres. Remember that this diagram shows *blood* lost, although other material is also lost from the womb lining during each period.

Women who have an IUD (intra-uterine device, or coil) fitted often find that they lose more than they did before it was fitted, while women on the Pill may find that they lose less.

WHAT CHANGES OCCUR IN THE VAGINA AND CERVIX?

As many women observe for themselves, the consistency of vaginal secretions varies with the menstrual cycle. Immediately after menstruation, for example, the vaginal secretions are scanty, while around ovulation, they are considerably thicker and whiter. The quality of these secretions can be used to indicate when you are ovulating, which you may wish to know if you want to conceive or to avoid conception. You might also want to know simply in order to find out more about your body and how it works. Many women are joining women's self-help health groups, where they can develop the techniques of self-examination and develop an understanding of their bodies. Recognizing our bodily changes is an important step in learning to deal with menstrual problems.

The changes in vaginal secretions are described in the accompanying chart (Table 2). If you are fortunate enough to have access to a microscope, then you can follow the changes in more detail. We know of some women who have bought themselves cheap microscopes so that they can better follow these changes. When the secretions from your vagina (preferably from quite high up inside the vagina) are swabbed onto a glass slide and allowed to dry, they form 'ferny' patterns around the time of ovulation (see Figure 3). The cells themselves, as seen under the microscope, also change with the cycle, as shown in Figure 4. Similar changes occur in the cells lining the mouth, and you might find these easier to see if you have a microscope. Cells from the lining of the mouth can be obtained by gently scraping the inside of your mouth with a finger-nail, and then wiping it across the slide.

DO THE SEX HORMONES AFFECT THE REST OF THE BODY?

All the changes described so far depend on the fluctuations of the hormones from the ovaries. We would expect the so-called sex hormones to affect the reproductive system – the uterus, Fallopian tubes and the vagina. But since they are carried in the blood to all parts of the body, they effect many other changes too. The breasts are affected, for example, especially just before menstruation, when

TABLE 2: THE EVENTS OF THE MENSTRUAL CYCLE

WHAT IS HAPPENING TO THE:			HOW SOME WOMEN SAY THEY FEEL:	
Uterus (Womb)	**Ovaries**	**Vagina**	**Pains**	**Moods**
Phase 1: Menstruation				
The lining starts to break down and is shed.	A new egg(ovum) begins to grow in one of the ovaries.	Vaginal secretions change from thick and white just before to scanty by the end.	Often cramps and/or low back pain, esp. at the beginning.	Tiredness to start with May feel more sexy
Phase 2: End of menstruation to about day 12 (follicular phase)*				
A new lining starts to form, but, as yet, it is not very thickly lined with blood vessels.	The new ovum becomes a 'graafian follicle' in which the ovum is surrounded by a sac of fluid.	Vaginal mucus is quite thin, and is alkaline. If allowed to dry on glass, it forms a 'fern' pattern (see diagram)		Often feel energetic, able to do things; outward going.
*Phase 3: Ovulation, about day 13-15**				
A new lining has developed during stage 2, ready to receive an ovum if it is fertilised.	Under influence of pituitary gland, ovum bursts out of follicle. Small amount of bleeding may accompany ovum release from ovary.	Mucus becomes very thin and stretchy. Larger quantity than usual. Readily shows fern pattern on glass.	A few women feel slight abdominal pain as the follicle ruptures.	Peak of energy. Some women feel sexier.
*Phase 4: The luteal phase: from day 15 to about day 25**				
The glands and blood-vessels become more tightly folded to receive and nourish a fertilised ovum if there is one.	Tissue left behind in ovary produces hormones which can maintain a pregnancy if necessary until the placentra is big enough to take over. These hormones cause the changes in the uterus.	Mucus is thick and white, containing cells from the vagina.		More inward-looking and reflective. Sometimes more tired. Time of lowered sex drive in some women.
Phase 5: From day 25 until the start of the next period*				
Glands and blood-vessels reach maximum folding. As hormone levels beginning to fall, the blood-vessels begin to constrict, ready for bleeding.	Hormone levels start to decline from the ovary. It is this which eventually brings about the bleeding.	As in previous stage though may become thicker.	May be some pain in the uterus, general body pains, nausea.	Many women report marked behaviour changes in this stage: irritability, depression, anxiety, etc.

* Dating the cycle starts from the *first* day of menstrual bleeding.

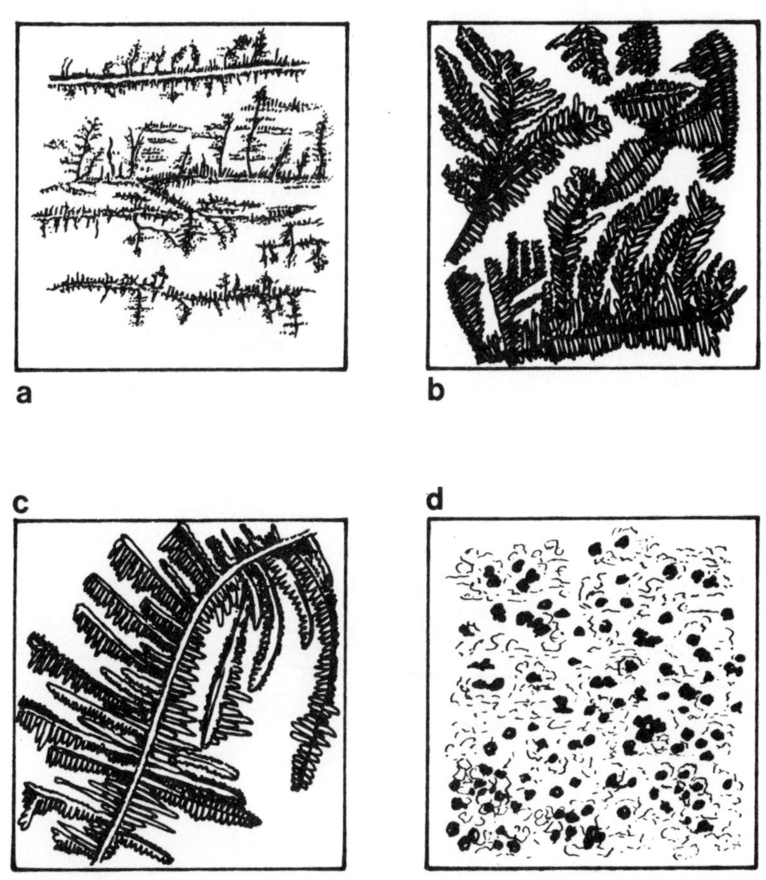

Figure 3: Changes in the appearance of vaginal mucus during the menstrual cycle.

If vaginal mucus is swabbed onto a microscope slide, its appearance changes with the stage of the menstrual cycle. (a) shows the appearance of mucus from early in the cycle, shortly after menstruation. (b) shows the appearance just before ovulation, about ten days after the start of the previous period (in some women having 28-day cycles). (c) shows mucus at the time of ovulation. In women who have not ovulated in that cycle, the mucus will probably remain like this until the next period. (d) shows mucus from the luteal phase (between ovulation and menstruation).

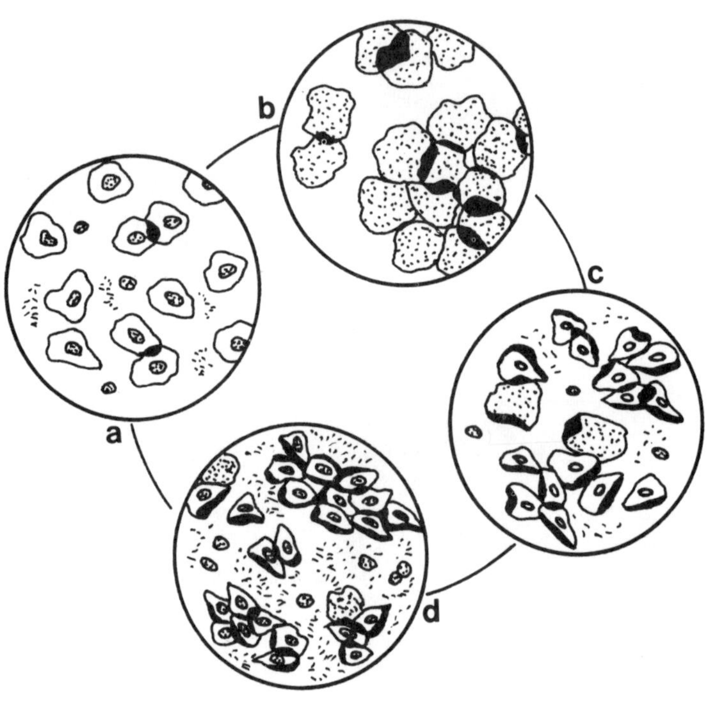

Figure 4: The Appearance of vaginal cells through the microscope

These are cells from the vaginal walls at different stages of the menstrual cycle. (a) shows cells from the second phase of the cycle, immediately after menstruation. (b) shows cells from the vagina just before ovulation. (c) shows cells shortly after ovulation, and (d) shows the appearance of cells in the luteal phase (between ovulation and menstruation).

they often swell somewhat. But many other bodily functions also change: such as carbohydrate metabolism (the rate at which you burn up sugars); sensitivity to smell; urine output; and the quantity of calcium in your blood. Some of these changes are listed in Table 1. Most of these go unnoticed. We only tend to notice those changes which in some way make us feel uncomfortable. Thus, we might complain about putting on some weight just before a period, but most women would not know whether or not they were more sensitive to smell.

All of these changes are, directly or indirectly, the result of changes in hormone levels. The slight increase in weight, for example, seems to be due to salt retention, which is in turn due to higher levels of oestrogen in the blood. Similarly, a heightened sensitivity to smell results from raised oestrogen levels coupled with low progestin levels around ovulation.

The general effects of the sex hormones on the body are perhaps most easily noticed during, and after, the menopause, when hormone levels are generally declining. Some doctors have claimed, for example, that declining oestrogens contribute to the bone-brittleness which characterises ageing. Because of this, many people have advocated taking artificial oestrogens to 'reverse' the changes to the body occurring during the menopause. But these are only reversed as long as a woman stays on the drug: some of the symptoms of the menopause (such as bone-brittleness) will return as soon as she comes off the drug. Hormone treatment might be useful for short-term treatment of such symptoms as severe hot flushes, which often do *not* reappear after the treatment is finished. Some doctors are fairly cautious about prescribing hormones for the menopause, except for short-term use while a woman experiences the most distressing symptoms. It is important to remember that synthetic hormones cannot truly replace a woman's natural hormones, and may well be hazardous if taken over many years. Although there has been a considerable amount of research into sex hormones, we still do not have enough information to determine whether long-term use of these hormones might have adverse effects on the body, including possible cancer risks. Since women now may expect to live a third of their lives after the menopause, they could end up taking artificial hormones for some time. The so-called 'hormone replacement therapy' is misleading, as it does not 'replace' the body's *natural* hormones. Women taking hormones are taking synthetic, not natural versions of the hormones.

HORMONES AND THE BRAIN

Hormones from the ovaries are also carried by the blood into the brain. Some scientists and doctors have, therefore, suggested that the unpleasant behavioural and mood changes which some women report just before a period are the result of imbalances of these hormones in the brain. The hormones are known to affect brain chemistry, and could, it is supposed, influence women's mood. This may well be why some women experience alterations in mood, such as depression or elation when they take the contraceptive Pill (which contains synthetic hormones).

The two types of hormones from the ovary – oestrogens and progestins – have different kinds of effect on brain activity. Oestrogens tend to increase brain activity slightly, while progestins tend to decrease it. This may be why some epileptics tend to have more fits during the premenstrual phase: during this phase, the levels of progestins are declining, and brain activity increases, thus making fits more likely. This effect on epilepsy may be the direct result of hormones influencing brain activity, or it may be an indirect effect of hormones on blood sugar levels, or on water retention – both of which can influence the level of activity of the brain. Scientists do not really know the answers yet.

CHANGING PERIODS

Although we have assumed that the average cycle length is twenty-eight days, it is obvious to most women that their cycles can vary in length quite considerably. During the first year or two after puberty, for instance, there may be long delays from one menstruation to the next. What kind of things, then, can trigger such variations in cycle length?

The two most obvious times in a woman's life when periods are irregular are puberty and menopause. Cycles in puberty are not very regular, as the body's rhythms are not fully established. During the first year or so, ovulation does not always occur, even if menstruation itself does: doctors call such cycles anovulatory cycles. Eventually, however, the menstrual cycle becomes stabilised, and menstruation usually occurs fairly regularly until pregnancy intervenes, or until the periods stop altogether at the menopause.

The menstrual cycle ceases to be regular during the menopausal years, as the important link between the pituitary and the ovaries begins to break down. It was once thought that menopause occurred as the supply of eggs ran out in the ovary. But it is now known that there are plenty of eggs left in the ovary at the time of menopause. Somehow, and it is not really known how, the hormonal link between the ovary and the pituitary winds down and eventually stops. Once the pituitary has stopped stimulating the ovaries, the ovaries produce little of their own hormones, and so no menstruation takes place. The most likely reason that we have a menopause at all is that old eggs are often faulty, and, if they were fertilised, would give rise to malformed babies. Menopause is nature's way of preventing this.

Between puberty and the menopause, the majority of women have fairly regular cycles, except, of course, during pregnancy and breast-feeding. Some women have very irregular cycles throughout their lives, and unfortunately little is known about why this occurs. It is only when a woman *suddenly* experiences irregular cycles, that irregularity *per se* should be a cause for concern. If her periods have always been regular, and then suddenly become irregular, she should see a doctor about it. For women who are always irregular, there is little need for concern, although it can be a nuisance for women wishing either to get pregnant or to avoid pregnancy.

The commonest cause of irregularity is stress. As the pituitary lies so close to the brain, it is subject to influences from it, such as emotional stress. If we are very anxious or worried about something, for instance starting a new job, the menstrual cycle can be interrupted or prolonged. Many women have discovered that the longer they worry about something, such as whether or not they are pregnant, the longer they have to wait until the period finally arrives.

SYNCHRONISING PERIODS

Women living together, or close friends, often find that their periods tend to arrive at the same time. It is not really known why this phenomenon occurs, but there is a possibility that it is due to faint odours (know to scientists as *pheromones*) of which we are unaware, but which are registered by our brains. These faint odours, which are emitted by all of us, may be sufficient to alter a woman's hormone pattern slightly, so that her cycle length becomes slightly longer or shorter until it coincides with that of her friend. Pheromones are well known in animals. In one research study, the experimenter found that female rats all began to synchronise their cycles as long as they were breathing the same air (which would carry the pheromones from one rat's cage to the next). Even when they could not see or hear each other, but were breathing air pumped from one cage to the next, their cycles synchronised. It is, of course, not yet certain whether similar pheromones operate to synchronise women's cycles: all that we know is that women do synchronise.

2 What is premenstrual tension?

In the last chapter, we referred to a number of bodily changes which accompany the menstrual cycle, most of which go unnoticed. In addition to these, many women find that their mood and feelings change too, especially during the premenstrual phase. Sometimes, just before a period, they feel irritable with the people around them, anxious, tired and depressed. The term *premenstrual tension* (PMT or premenstrual syndrome) is used by doctors to describe all those negative feelings which women say they feel just before a period. Some doctors also include physical changes, such as bloatedness, as symptoms of premenstrual tension.

Much research has been carried out in recent years into the changes which women report at particular phases of the menstrual cycle. Not all of it is particularly good research, and some of it has been criticised by other researchers. But we can draw some conclusions from it. For example, from studies in which women were asked to fill out a questionnaire describing the symptoms of the premenstrual phase which they experienced, it seems that the changes which women report most frequently are as follows:

Pain: including muscle stiffness, headaches, migraine, cramps, backache, fatigue, general aches and pains.
Changes in concentration: including insomnia, forgetfulness, confusion, lowered judgements, distractability.
Other behavioural changes: including lowered work performance, lower efficiency.
'Autonomic reactions': including dizziness, cold sweats, nausea, vomiting, hot flushes, fainting.
Water retention: including swelling of abdomen and ankles, weight gain, swelling and painful breasts.
Mood change: including crying, anxiety, irritability, depression, tension.

The way that these are grouped together reflects the way researchers found that the symptoms occurred together. In other words, they found that women who experienced, say, changes in concentration, would tend to experience most other changes in this category.

Apart from these, many other conditions are more likely to arise just before a period, such as acne, mouth ulcers, epilepsy, asthma, and other allergic disorders. Women may also find that they dream more than usual, and may feel sexier than at other times of the cycle.

Readers may recognise some of these changes as events which they, or women they know, experience. They are the commonest changes which have been reported by women in studies using questionnaires. As we have said, research of this nature is not always good research, and it has been criticised: partly because people often fill out questionnaires in ways that they think they should, rather than in ways which indicate how they actually feel. So questionnaire-based research into the menstrual cycle may indicate only what women *believe* about the menstrual cycle and its changes, rather than indicating their true moods and feelings. Many women in our society are brought up to expect mood changes before a period; it is also possible that some women experience mood changes because they expect to.

The fact that questionnaire-based research may not always be completely trustworthy is not the same as saying that premenstrual tension does not exist. We may be dubious about some of the studies on it, but we are sure that PMT does exist, and that it can cause considerable misery for some women. A number of people still maintain that PMT is 'all in the mind'. This is not only extremely unhelpful to those women who suffer, but it is disparaging and untrue. Those who take such an unhelpful view may insist that the answer lies in such things as having a baby/having another baby/ getting a job/getting a better job/getting a husband/settling down and so on. Suggestions of this kind made to women suffering from 'women's problems' are endless. And they are absurd and unhelpful.

It is equally silly to say, as some doctors have done, that the only women who suffer from PMT are those who are 'neurotic'. All kinds of women find that they experience physical and mental changes which cause some discomfort premenstrually: this discomfort is not the prerogative of any particular type of woman.

PMT AND WOMEN WORKING

Most of us have read at some time or another that women's performance at work may be adversely affected by premenstrual changes. Indeed, this is sometimes stated as an excuse for not employing women in particular jobs. But is it true?

A few women – those affected by particularly debilitating changes in the premenstrual phase – may find that their ability to carry out some aspects of their day-to-day work is impaired premenstrually. Most of these women soon learn to cope effectively with this problem by organising their more difficult work (if it is at all possible) at other times. More routine work, for example, might be carried out during this time, and work requiring more concentration and care might be kept for other times when they feel more capable of it.

It is important to remember that very few of us are employed in work which *continually* requires high levels of concentration, and which cannot be reorganised: the majority of us are in work which requires us to concentrate in short bursts. Thus it does not really matter much if there are one or two days on which we feel less able to concentrate. More to the point, there has been some research which shows that in women academics, who presumably have to concentrate on their studies, work performance and concentration are actually better during the premenstrual phase, not worse. The people who did the research have suggested that, because these women *expect* to feel worse premenstrually and to be less able to concentrate, they tried harder than usual.

It is also important to remember that when these papers refer to women suffering from 'lowered work performance' premenstrually, they often fail to take into account that women presumably have a 'raised work performance' at other times in their cycles. For those women who do feel that they suffer from concentration problems premenstrually, it is vital to remember this.

For most women, then, the ability to concentrate and to carry out particular jobs is *not* especially affected during the premenstrual phase. There are, however, a few women for whom the premenstrual phase represents problems. For these women, the best solution seems to be a reorganisation of the workload within the demands of the job.

PMT AND THE FAMILY

PMT is often referred to as a potential disrupter of family life. Women suffering from premenstrual irritability often take it out on children, sometimes violently. They may become 'accident-prone', or allow their children to have an accident. Obviously an anxious and irritable mother is not likely to promote harmony within the family. It is for these reasons that many women seek help from the medical profession, or from books such as this.

It is interesting that it is only relatively recently that PMT was seen as a problem. Although doctors throughout the ages have written of women's changing moods, it was not until the end of the last century and the beginning of the twentieth century that premenstrual mood changes were seen as a problem which might require medical help. Partly this was due to the discovery of the hormones, which enabled doctors to work out some of the mysteries of the menstrual cycle. It might also have had something to do with the changing status of the family. For most of human history, people have tended to live in larger groups than we now do: families consisted of more than one generation, and may have included too aunts and uncles, all living close together. In such an environment, it seems likely that if any one woman was feeling bad-tempered because of PMT, then no one need take too much notice because there were plenty of other people to buffer the effects of her temper. But the last one hundred and fifty years have seen dramatic changes in the family. It is now considered normal to live in a nuclear family, in which a woman spends much of her time alone interacting with her children and with no one else. Small wonder that premenstrual mood changes take on so much importance.

OTHER PREMENSTRUAL CHANGES

Apart from the changes in mood outlined above, there have also been reports that women are more likely to commit criminal offences, to commit suicide, or to be admitted to a psychiatric hospital when they are premenstrual than at any other time of the cycle. These predictions were taken very seriously during the nineteenth century, when doctors would issue dire warnings to other doctors about the risk of 'premenstrual madness'.

What these reports mean is not that otherwise perfectly sane and happy individuals suddenly become psychiatric cases, or suddenly become suicidally depressed. Rather they mean that women who were depressed or unhappy anyway felt considerably worse during the premenstrual phase. Peter Redgrove and Penelope Shuttle, in their book, *The Wise Wound,* have described it as the time when women 'tell it like it really is' – when they become more honest with themselves. That is, a woman who is depressed might be able to suppress the real reasons for her depression, even to herself, for most of the cycle but is less able to do so premenstrually. Perhaps the woman who shouts at her husband during the premenstrual phase is really trying to say that she has grievances against him which she successfully suppresses at other times. Certainly the authors of this book have both recognised that if we are generally unhappy, the reasons for that unhappiness seem much clearer, much more obvious just before a period is due. And that clarity can make us feel unhappier still. Not everyone agrees with this view, but it is an interesting one that we might all consider.

Other events are more likely to occur just before a period. Children are apparently more likely to be kept away from school, or taken to see the family doctor while their mother is premenstrual. More accidents can occur when a woman is premenstrual. Some women say that they are more likely to drop things, to slip and fall, to knock things over. No one really knows whether or not this is related to hormones: it is also possible, for example, that these women who feel that they are more accident-prone in fact *notice* minor accidents more just before a period, rather than that they actually have more such accidents. Unfortunately there has been very little research into accident-proneness and the menstrual cycle.

We began this chapter by outlining some of the mood changes which women say they experience. We, and most of the women we have talked to, have experienced some of these. We know that there is not enough *good* research into mood or behavioural changes and their relation to the menstrual cycle.

But this does not alter the fact that most women experience some of these changes at some time in their lives. For a few women, these changes are frequent, and very severe – often with disastrous consequences. For them, child-abuse, injuries and accidents, attempts at suicide can be among the consequences of drastic mood swings with the menstrual cycle. Doctors dealing with patients who suffer from such severe, and often incapacitating, changes have suggested theories of the possible causes of PMT. Some claim that the various symptoms are due to this or that hormone, and others claim that most symptoms of premenstrual tension are psychological. For most women the truth lies somewhere in between.

3 Causes of premenstrual tension

There have been nearly as many theories of the causes of premenstrual tension as there are symptoms of it. We will outline the major theories in this chapter, before going on to outline the treatments which are suggested by these theories. We must point out, however, that they are *theories:* medical science still knows relatively little about the biology of the menstrual cycle, and about the causes of premenstrual distress. Probably no one of these theories is the true one, although all may have some truth in them. One theory may apply to some women some of the time, but not to others. Or maybe premenstrual tension results from a combination of several factors acting simultaneously. Some of these theories are specifically medical ones.

Until the nineteenth century, doctors tended to believe that the womb was the seat of women's troubles. For many centuries, it was believed that the womb actually wandered about in the body, causing all kinds of ills and making women behave in strange, unpredictable ways. Now that hormones have been discovered (they were discovered at the beginning of this century), it is hormones which are often thought to be the cause of women's unpredictability. This might be called the 'raging hormone theory': that is, the belief that women are the hapless victims of raging hormones which dictate their bodily and psychological state, and from which there is no escape. This implies that little can be done about it, except by giving women drugs to stop the 'raging'. Apart from the fact that this view ignores much of what is known about women's attitudes to menstruation, this theory has also been used as an excuse to prevent women from having responsible jobs. The claim is that, as women become helpless victims of their hormones once a month, they cannot be relied on to make sensible decisions. Karen Paige, a psychologist who has studied premenstrual mood changes, quotes an American doctor who, in 1970, had this to say about the possibility of having a woman as bank manager, or as President of the United States:

> 'If you had an investment in a bank, you wouldn't want the president of the bank making a loan under those raging hormonal influences at that particular period. Suppose we had a President of the White House, a menopausal woman president, who had to make the decision of the Bay of Pigs, which was, of course, a bad one, or about the Russian contretemps with Cuba at that time?

A woman might well have made a sensible decision. But if she had made a bad one, (as even American presidents do sometimes) the doctor could always tell the world that women cannot be trusted – because of their 'raging hormones'.

It is, of course, undeniably true that a woman's hormones wax and wane during the course of a menstrual cycle, as we have discussed earlier. It is also true that the menstrual cycle is, for many women, accompanied by feelings which they do not like (or which other people do not like!). No one knows for sure, however, whether these hormone swings actually *cause* the mood changes or whether they just happen to coincide with them. There is reason to believe, in fact, that the hormone swings have rather less to do with mood swings than is popularly supposed.

MENSTRUAL BELIEFS: SHAME AND SECRECY

Although attitudes are slowly beginning to change, many women still feel that they are unclean when they are menstruating, and that this is a cause for shame. It is a common attitude, and exists among many different peoples of the world. In some societies, menstruating women are feared, and are thought to bring bad luck to others (especially to men) whom they touch. They are often thought to make young plants wither, to make food go bad, to bring death. As a result, many societies expect menstruating women to segregate themselves into special huts for the duration of their period. Centuries ago, people in Europe believed that menstruating women would make milk go sour, would dull razors, would turn meat poisonous, and destroy insects.

Readers may feel that what people did centuries ago, or what they do in other societies today, is not necessarily relevant to those of us who live in Western industrialised society: after all, surely we do not treat menstruating women in such ways? Unfortunately, to some extent, we still do. There are still many people in the Western world who believe that meat touched by a menstruating woman will 'go off': that menstruating women should stay away from plant nurseries in case the young plants wither: that menstruating women may be susceptible to attack by wild animals: and that they should not cook because the food might spoil. These are beliefs which are held by people in parts of Europe and America: they are not beliefs of people from societies alien to our own. It does not matter that such beliefs are scientifically untrue: the fact is that some people think they are true. Even those who might consider themselves to be fairly sophisticated still harbour beliefs about the impurity of menstruation. Perhaps related to the feeling that menstrual blood is impure is the idea that you should keep it hidden. Many women refuse to talk about it, and all advertisements for pads and tampons emphasise the secrecy. We are told that such-and-such a product is the only sanitary protection that you can be sure will not give your secret away.

Periods are generally viewed with some distaste in our society. Women often refer to having periods as the 'curse', 'feeling poorly', 'that awful time of the month', or simply 'It'. Menstruation is usually spoken about in words which imply that we do not like it very much: if, that is, it is spoken about at all. Many women (and men) avoid talking about the subject if at all possible.

Women often feel that they are unclean during menstruation, or are told by other people that they are unclean, and feel embarrassed about it: many men, for example, refuse to have sex with a menstruating woman, as they feel that she is 'dirty' – even though most women tend to feel quite sexy during their periods. The idea that menstrual blood is dirty, or even dangerous, has remained a very persistent one.

Another persistent idea is that of 'bad blood'. One of the authors of this book was told, when she was young, never to swim or have a bath during her periods, as it would 'dam up the bad blood inside'. Menstrual blood, of course, is not 'bad blood' that must be got rid of at all costs: it is simply the lining of the womb which was prepared for pregnancy if fertilisation had occurred. Nor,, if a woman has light periods, does this mean that something awful has happened. Some women believe that if they have a light period, then the blood must have gone somewhere else. This is not true. A light period simply means that the hormones from the ovary have not built up as thick a lining as usual – so there is less to come away at menstruation. Going swimming during a period is, in fact, an excellent idea, provided that the water is not too cold, as the exercise is good for menstrual cramps.

Those women who feel that the blood must go 'somewhere' may become anxious if their flow is less than usual, as they see menstruation as necessary to remove the bad blood. In one research study, in a small country village, it turned out that those women who believed this were the ones who were most likely to suffer from premenstrual tension: they felt huge, bloated, and 'poisoned' with the blood which they believed had been building up since the last period. Menstruation, they said, was a relief from the tension as it 'got rid of' the bad blood. For these women, what they *believed* seemed to be related to how they *felt* before a period was due. Those women who did not share these beliefs about bad blood did not apparently suffer in the same way from premenstrual tension.

There is a certain amount of evidence that what you *expect* to feel premenstrually, is in fact what you do feel: it becomes a self-fulfilling prophecy. This is not saying that one is 'simply imagining it', or is 'neurotic'. Many kinds of illness and distress are profoundly altered by what people believe about the illness. One woman researcher found that women's reports of how they felt just before a period were almost identical with men's reports of how they *thought* women felt. She suggested that women may describe whatever they have been taught to expect, and men share this expectation. If we are told that it is normal for women to be irritable and difficult before a period, and we happen to feel irritable one day, what is more natural than to blame it on the forthcoming period? The irritability may not in fact be *caused* by the impending period, but because we know that the period is due, and we believe that women often get irritable at that time, we are likely to believe that this day of irritability is caused by the menstruation which follows it. If we get irritable at any other time of the cycle, then we do not have anything obvious to blame it on. Doctors have no real idea as to how many women who suffer premenstrually do so because they expect to suffer, and how many suffer because of some genuine hormonal problem.

Keeping a menstrual calender can be a useful way of understanding the menstrual cycle, as well as enabling a woman to determine whether she really does get moody only during the premenstrual phase. By noting down the days on which she feels miserable, bitchy or whatever, a woman can determine whether these days have any cyclical pattern. If they do not, then the mood swings are not PMT. If they do tend to occur always at the same time, a few days before a period is due, then we can describe it as PMT, although it tells us nothing about the possible cause.

So far, we have implied that PMT may not always be caused by hormones, but what is the evidence for this? There is some suggestive evidence, although (as happens frequently in research), there is nothing definite. Firstly, if PMT were all due to hormones, then we might expect those women on the Pill to suffer from few symptoms, since their own hormones are suppressed by the constant levels of hormones in the Pill. Secondly, we might also expect those women who have a hysterectomy without their ovaries being removed (some hysterectomies involve removing the ovaries as well), to experience cyclical mood changes, since they still have their ovaries and ovarian hormones.

There is some evidence that neither of these things occur. For example, there is evidence that women on the Pill do experience cyclic fluctuations in mood, especially in the premenstrual phase, and that many women whose wombs, but not ovaries, have been removed do not experience any cyclic mood changes. If women without wombs but with ovaries do *not* usually experience mood swings, then we could conclude that the premenstrual mood swings are more related to anticipation of bleeding from the womb than to hormone activity.

Finally, apart from beliefs about menstruation itself, we must point out that our society seems to dislike, condemn and perhaps fear change and inconsistency. This may be due to the nature of the demands made on people in our culture. This emphasis on consistency and demand for stability in mood and functioning affects men too, of course, but women are affected in more specific ways, since we have more regular and obvious signs of change in the form of our monthly bleeding. (Recent research has shown that men also have regular bodily rhythms although these are not necessarily a month long, but that they are less obvious than those of women.)

Most of the written studies of the menstrual cycle seem to imply that women ought not to undergo changes, that we should never be irritable. Such studies seem to focus too on the negative aspects of the cycle – women's complaints of irritability and lack of concentration, for instance rather than any positive aspects. Many women themselves focus on these negative aspects. But then they are likely to see their doctor about those premenstrual changes which make them feel less efficient. Hence it is depression, irritability, insomnia, forgetfulness, and so on which may persuade a woman to seek medical help.

While these are clearly distressing changes, we should not forget that there are also times of the menstrual cycle when we can experience *positive* changes. Many women find, for example, that there are feelings of heightened energy and creativeness at certain phases; feelings which they can often use to their advantage. For most women, there is a noticeable feeling of tremendous energy, which usually occurs in the first half of the cycle, often around ovulation. Even in the premenstrual phase, when so many of these negative feelings may occur, there are some changes which can be pleasurable. A number of women have found that they feel sexier around the time of menstruation, for instance. The incidence of dreaming-sleep seems to increase too, which is seen by many people as a positive aspect of menstrual cycle changes.

It is often helpful to women who experience negative changes within their cycles to try to come to terms with the fact that women *do* change, and to try to plan their lives accordingly. This means *accepting* the fluctuations, even discovering that they might have benefits. We explore this in more detail in the next chapter.

GENERAL PSYCHOLOGICAL EFFECTS OF HORMONES

One view of hormones and their effect on the menstrual cycle is that the hormones involved have a *general* effect on the brain, and hence on a woman's mood, especially where she has negative attitudes to menstruation. This theory is based on a notion of general arousal.

In one scientific study of stimulant drugs and their effects on people's moods, researchers found that people who had received the drug claimed to have felt different things, according to the mood of the people around them. The drug simply produced a state of arousal, or excitement, but if the people around them were feeling and behaving as though they were sad, then the person who had had the drug also felt sad. Similarly, if people around were laughing and behaving happily, the person who had been given the drug reported being happy. In other words, although the drug is acting to make someone more aroused or excited, how they interpret their arousal depends on their immediate environment.

This has led some researchers into the menstrual cycle to suggest that a similar thing happens in PMT. The hormone changes themselves could have a general arousing effect on the body: but if a woman feels negative about menstruation, and has been brought up to believe that most women feel irritable prior to menstruation, then it is likely that she will perceive the arousal as irritability, anxiety or depression, as this is what she will expect to feel. Women who feel positive about menstruation, and who look forward to it on the other hand, might perceive premenstrual arousal as elation and happiness. We are not very likely to hear about such women, of course, since women are not very likely to complain, or to consult a doctor if they feel elated premenstrually.

This kind of theory implies that the hormones from the ovaries *are* involved, but not in a direct way (ie. the hormones do not directly determine a specific mood, such as anxiety or irritability). It also implies that a woman's beliefs about menstruation affect her experiences of it. The hormones are, according to this theory, causing a general change, but it is the attitude of the woman concerned which brings about the specific changes of depression, anxiety and so on. This might help to explain why so many different symptoms are reported for PMT.

Although hormonal 'imbalances' may well be involved in PMT, it seems unlikely to us that this is the whole story. Girls growing up in our society (and boys too), soon learn that menstruation is not quite 'nice', that it is often painful, that they may put on weight, or get more spots than usual, that they may become irritable or depressed. All these are part of the folklore of menstruation which is taught, directly or indirectly, to young women. It would be surprising indeed if these beliefs did not contribute in some way to the feelings which women have about menstruation. How we feel about menstruation and premenstrual changes probably has as much to do with our culture as it has to do with biology.

PHYSICAL THEORIES

Although there is mounting evidence that beliefs and attitudes contribute to premenstrual problems, a number of people have advocated theories which imply that the cause of PMT is a straightforward hormonal imbalance, which can usually be treated quite easily by prescribing hormonal drugs to the woman concerned. It may well be that some women suffering from PMT have an imbalance of certain hormones, but it is not certain that *all* such women have hormone problems. Unfortunately, few doctors have the time or patience to talk to women complaining of PMT, so that hormonal theories often seem to many doctors to be the best answer. These physical theories are, therefore, those on which most medical treatment is based, though treating PMT as a purely medical phenomenon, to be treated only with suitable drugs, may not always be the most appropriate answer. We shall discuss the various theories on which drug treatment is based.

Imbalances of Oestrogen and Progesterone

The first of these theories is that those women who suffer bad premenstrual problems suffer from an imbalance of oestrogens and progesterone. This theory was first suggested by Dr Katherina Dalton, who distinguished between *spasmodic* and *congestive dysmenorrhoea* (pain associated with menstruation). Spasmodic dysmenorrhoea is sharp, cramping pains usually associated with the bleeding itself, while congestive is the nagging pains, accompanied by lethargy and water retention, which characterises premenstrual tension for many women. Dr Dalton believes that congestive pain results from too little progesterone in the second half of the cycle, and spasmodic from too little oestrogen. She claims to have had some success in treating women with bad premenstrual tension, by giving them progesterone injections or suppositories. A number of synthetic progestins such as *didroprogesterone* are now available in place of pure progesterone (which can only be given as injection or suppository) for treating PMT.

In one study conducted at a London teaching hospital, doctors also found that progesterone relieved premenstrual distress in about 30 per cent of sufferers. However, although there is evidence that it works in some cases, many other doctors are sceptical. Some who have studied the menstrual cycle have found that PMT sufferers do not always have low levels of progesterone. It is also known that some women who appear to have relatively low levels of progesterone do not suffer from PMT problems at all.

People studying the menstrual cycle often disagree about which treatments work and which do not. This may be because it is not always clear what symptoms they are trying to treat. There are many bodily changes associated with the menstrual cycle, as we have already pointed out.

Dr Dalton's theory has been criticised by a number of people, but it remains a theory which has prompted a considerable amount of research into PMT. More importantly, it was Dr Dalton's work which finally broke the silence about PMT in medical journals.

Prolactin

Prolactin is another hormone secreted by the pituitary gland at the base of the brain. In mammals, such as humans, its chief role is in stimulating milk production by the mammary glands for suckling the young. However, it is also known to affect water and mineral balance in many animals. This has led some doctors to suggest that prolactin plays a part in PMT changes, causing water retention and breast enlargement. The amount of prolactin in blood is maximum around ovulation, and remains high during the second half of the cycle, until the next period. It is during this time that some women gain weight. Doctors have tried out a new drug which lowers the amount of prolactin in blood during the second half of the menstrual cycle, and which seems to make some women feel less bloated.

Adrenal hormones

The adrenal glands, situated above the kidneys, produce several hormones. One of these, *aldosterone,* controls mineral balance in the body, and so has been implicated in premenstrual tension. The water retention that many women complain of just before a period results from mineral retention (especially sodium). Since aldosterone affects the amount and distribution of sodium in the body, it could lead to water retention, and so might be involved in PMT. This theory is related to the progesterone-deficiency theory, since progesterone tends to inhibit the action of aldosterone. Thus, if you have low levels of progesterone, you may be more sensitive to the mineral and water-retaining effects of aldosterone. Aldosterone is essential to your body, and your body cannot work without it, but it is possible that some people are more sensitive to its water-retaining effects than others.

Thyroid Hormones

There has been a suggestion that the thyroid gland, situated in the neck, is in some way involved in premenstrual changes such as lethargy and loss of appetite. However, this idea does not seem to have gained much acceptance among doctors, and there are few who would recommend drugs which would alter thyroid output solely for premenstrual tension.

Brain chemistry

Because the steroid hormones get into the brain, they can affect brain chemistry. Many women find that if they are depressed anyway, then the depression is likely to get worse premenstrually. This might be because depression can bring about a temporary alteration in brain chemistry, which might become exacerbated as the hormone levels change during the menstrual cycle.

Brain chemistry is immensely complex and poorly understood, so we will not go into too much detail here. There are, however, some drugs which can alter brain chemistry in such a way that some premenstrual changes are altered. The simplest of these is vitamin B6 (*pyridoxine*). It is thought that the oestrogen/progesterone balance in some contraceptive pills, and premenstrually, may increase some women's requirements of this vitamin, beyond the amount which can be obtained in a normal diet. The effects of this vitamin deficiency can include depression, which can often be corrected by taking tablets of the vitamin. Doctors have been trying out vitamin B6 for treating PMT, as we discuss in the next chapter.

All tranquillisers and anti-depressants work by altering brain chemistry. However, most of these need to be taken over long periods of time for them to work effectively, especially the anti-depressants. As PMT occurs only for relatively short periods, such long-term drugs are often less suitable for treating it than, say, vitamin B6. A few women find that tranquillisers taken in the last few days before a period helps them, although this seems quite a drastic treatment so we would not recommend it for most women. More importantly, if one of your premenstrual changes is to become lethargic, tranquillisers are only likely to make it worse! Whether or not to take such drugs should, of course, be a woman's choice, as we discuss further in the next chapter.

All these theories, as we have indicated, have their supporters. A woman's GP may well support one of these theories, or s/he may not believe in PMT at all. There seems to be evidence for and against each of them: perhaps all of them are partially true. When you have read this book, and if you feel that you require help from your doctor for PMT, make sure that you are familiar with the different ideas of what causes PMT, so that you can discuss it fully with your doctor, and decide what you can do. Make sure, too, that your doctor does not try to give you a treatment which you feel that you would rather not have, just because s/he supports a particular theory: it is up to *you* to decide ultimately. Many GPs do not have the time to keep completely up to date with all the research and theories, so it may help if you take this book along with you.

We hope that readers too do not feel too bewildered by all these facts and conflicting ideas. We wish we were in a position to tell you exactly what happens during the menstrual cycle, and why PMT occurs. Premenstrual tension is, however, very complex, and little understood. Much depends – as we have frequently emphasised – on the individual woman and her feelings and physiology. Our personal view is that the causes of PMT are likely to be many and varied, and are likely to include both hormones and attitudes. Even for one particular woman, one menstrual cycle is not necessarily the same as another. You might, for example, have breast soreness one month, and depression the next.

We now turn to different kinds of treatment available to PMT sufferers. In the spirit of our view that attitudes are at least as important as physiology, we start off by dealing with attitudes and feelings. We also consider that much can be gained from self-help, so our discussion of treatments is centred on things which women can do for themselves. But we also know that some women will not find self-help to be sufficient, and will find that their PMT is only adequately relieved by drugs. So, finally, we discuss each of the drug treatments obtainable through doctors.

4 Dealing with premenstrual tension

There are many ways of dealing with premenstrual tension. Some women find that they can simply ignore it, that their problems are not so severe as to cause much distress. Others find it impossible to ignore, as they experience changes which they find very distressing and which can disrupt their lives. It is not always easy to decide just how bad your problems are, as they may vary markedly from month to month. Dealing with PMT can be made more difficult too, if other people persist in telling you how awful you are premenstrually! It is not always easy to ignore these comments, especially if they are made by someone close to you: and it is particularly difficult not to feel guilty about it if your children appear to be affected. But it is most important to remember that in the first instance it is *you* who is the sufferer. Your behaviour may become unpredictable to those around you, but it is also you who has to cope with the guilt if your children, for instance, suffer from these changes.

The first step in learning to deal with PMT is to learn to accept that you *do* change, and to encourage those people closest to you to accept this too. Most people have very little understanding of the events of the menstrual cycle, and consequently have very little tolerance of changes which accompany it. You can help yourself a great deal by talking to your lover/husband/friends/children about your menstruation and what it means to you. Women are not like men (or rather as men prefer to think men are!), since women's bodies undergo clear rhythmic changes in the form of the menstrual cycle. Your work, children, or other adults, may expect you to be as unchanging as possible, to be highly predictable. Learning to accept, and to understand our rhythms is not necessarily easy, as we have all grown up in a society which encourages shame and secrecy about menstruation.

There are aspects of this changingness which we may well feel we do not like: irritability is a good example. But we must remember that changingness also brings changes which we can enjoy. Thus it is not so much the changing itself that women worry about: it is those mood swings which adversely affect other people.

Some women, especially in women's self-help health groups, are beginning to try to understand the changes of the menstrual cycle better, so that they can overcome many of the problems associated with different moods. A few women have come to feel positive about their menstruation: they see it as a time when they are more 'in tune' with their bodily cycles, with nature. They see it as an important experience which reaffirms their womanhood. The authors of this book have come to realise that the more we try to throw off the shame, guilt and secrecy surrounding menstruation, the more we come to enjoy it – and, more important, the less we suffer from pains and problems. We know that such changes may well not happen to every woman who tries to exorcise the shame within herself, but we believe that confronting that shame and guilt is a necessary first step towards understanding – and liking – our bodies better.

FOLLOWING OUR CHANGES

Self-examination on a regular basis is one way of beginning to understand ourselves a little better. Self-examination of the vagina and cervix with a plastic speculum can teach you a great deal about how your body changes cyclically, as well as providing you with information about the health of your vagina. If you need further information about self-examination, you can consult the books listed in the appendix, or you can contact a woman's self-help group or a 'well-woman clinic': there are several of these around the country (see p.68).

By noting down any physical changes in your body, and the way you are feeling generally, you can build up a 'profile' of your menstrual cycle, and the changes which characterise it for you. This can help you to understand it better (see pp 15–19 for the physical changes which you might notice). Through this understanding, by learning to think more positively about menstruation in general, you may well find that some of your premenstrual distress becomes less distressing.

DISCUSSION/CONSCIOUSNESS-RAISING

This may seem a very strange place to start. However, several women have found that the more they talk about it, the less distressing their premenstrual tension becomes. So 'discussion' is, in fact, worth talking about here.

Discussing premenstrual tension with other women can be helpful, provided that the overall aim of such discussion is to go beyond merely comparing notes on the severity of changes experienced. Simply swapping horror stories rarely does much beyond the comfort of knowing that there is someone who suffers more than you do! The 'consciousness-raising group' is an important part of the Women's Liberation Movement, and consists of a small group of women who meet regularly to discuss their ideas freely with each other, and to develop their awareness of the problems faced by women in this society. Menstruation and premenstrual distress might be a particularly good topic for such a group to discuss. Discussion could centre on the effects of the menstrual taboo (which we briefly considered earlier), and how deeply each woman is affected by the negative experiences of menstruation.

By learning to talk more openly about menstruation, women in these dicussion groups might begin to feel more free to talk about it to other people, and raise their understanding too. Although women sometimes do talk about menstruation with close women friends, it is not so long since our grandmothers' days when it was taboo to talk about it at all, unless one used euphemisms such as 'feeling unwell', or 'off-days'. Even now, we tend to *apologise* for the fact that we menstruate: comments like 'I'm sorry, I'm run down – it's the curse', or 'I'm sorry, I can't come out, I've got my period' are still common. Perhaps one aim of a consciousness-raising group should be to overcome this apologising attitude. We should not have to apologise for the fact that we are women.

Working in a group can also be useful for developing techniques, such as massage for period pains; and for dispelling myths, eg. that we should not go swimming during menstruation. However you decide to organise your group is obviously a matter of choice: much depends on who is in it, and how well you know each other. A group of caring women can be very supportive and cohesive.

The outcome of such a group might well be that the women in it no longer feel particularly distressed by menstrual problems: indeed, we know of many women for whom that experience has been true. Even for those women whose distress is severe, it can be a great source of comfort and help to be able to turn to other women.

NATURAL REMEDIES: LOOKING TO YOUR DIET AND HEALTH

Much of the food we eat today is relatively low in vitamins and minerals as a result of processing, which removes many essential nutrients. Consequently, many of us may be getting insufficient nourishment from the food we eat. There is very little known about the relationship, if any, between nutrition and menstrual problems, largely because very little research has yet been conducted. Nevertheless, taking care of our diet may well provide some help to women suffering from PMT or other menstrual problems. Making sure that we eat well-balanced diets, with plenty of fresh vegetables and fruit, as well as avoiding too much greasy or processed food is important. It is all too easy to reach for processed for convenience, especially if children are around (who all too often seem to prefer convenience foods!), but they do little for our health. Wheatgerm and wholemeal bread, for example, should be eaten instead of white bread, as these contain more of the important B vitamins.

Meat contains a number of additives, including some hormones, which are supplied to the animal in its feed to fatten it up quickly. Meat-eaters are hence ingesting small quantities of these additives at every meal, while vegetarians are less likely to do so. No-one knows the possible harmful effects of ingesting these hormones over long periods of time. It is quite possible that they could contribute to women's menstrual problems. It has been claimed, for example, that vegetarians tend to suffer less from menstrual cramps than do meat-eaters.

As so little is known about the effects of eating processed food over long periods of time, we can only hazard guesses about their effects on women's bodies. But it hardly seems likely that food additives (which are found in all processed foods) can do us much good, and they may well do us harm.

There are several dietary changes which you might make if you suffer from specific problems premenstrually. We can't say that they will definitely help: much depends on your own body chemistry. If you do not wish to take drugs, but would rather overcome your menstrual problems more gently, then you may wish to try dietary changes.

If bloatedness is a problem, for example, you might try a number of different things. A few days before you expect to start feeling bloated (if it is predictable), you should try to cut down your intake of both fluid and salt (which includes that used in cooking). In addition, it is helpful to eat foods, or to take herbal remedies, which are naturally diuretic (ie. which increase your urine output and decrease fluid retention). Among foods which have this property are: cranberries, aubergines, artichokes, asparagus, cucumber, parsley (fresh), parsnips, strawberries, watercress and watermelon. You could also try drinking strong coffee in small quantities.

The bloatedness is usually accompanied by a retention of sodium (we usually refer to this as salt retention), and a depletion of potassium, as the body tends to exchange sodium for potassium and vice versa. Thus, in addition to restricting your salt intake, try eating foods rich in potassium, such as bananas, tomatoes, soya beans and oranges.

If you are a person who likes alcoholic drinks, you might try to get hold of some sloe gin (or make it yourself), as the sloe berry is a natural diuretic. Drinkers should, of course, avoid such long drinks as beer, and turn instead to short drinks such as spirits or wine (as long as you don't overdo it!).

Bloatedness may also be associated with calcium deficiency, or with a temporary pyridoxine (vitamin B6) deficiency. Making sure that you have enough of these may have other benefits. For example, many women claim that by taking calcium tablets and/or ensuring that they eat enough calcium-rich foods (such as green vegetables and dairy foods of all kinds) for the ten days before a period, the period becomes less painful, and there are fewer headaches associated with menstruation. Taking extra pyridoxine can help too. Foods which are rich in this vitamin are wholewheat, brown rice, walnuts, almonds, liver, avocado pears.

Some women have also tried ammonium chloride for bloating. This substance can be obtained from chemists, and is not harmful in small quantities. It is known to be a diuretic, and so can relieve bloating to some extent. It is far cheaper to buy it as simple ammonium chloride, rather than in the form of expensive tablets (you would need to take about a teaspoon a day). There *are* special tablets, marketed by an astute drug company, which claim to get rid of excess premenstrual water: they consist of nothing more than ammonium chloride plus a little caffeine – the stimulant in tea and coffee.

A number of people now turn to herbal remedies for ill-health, believing them to be gentler, and safer, than conventional drugs. This is to some extent true, and indeed most herbs known to medieval herbalists are known to contain small quantities of active compounds. Most of them do work, provided that they are taken over a long enough period of time. The active ingredients of herbal medicines work gently on the body, but need to be taken for a long period of time, whereas the concentrated ingredients of modern drugs work faster, and so do not have to be taken for so long. Many modern drugs are, in fact, made from plant extracts: the best known example being digitalis, given for heart complaints, and extracted from foxgloves.

However, while herbs are gentle in moderate doses, you should remember that most of them do contain ingredients which act on the body, and should be treated with caution. Don't become addicted just because herbal teas taste nice. Anything taken in excess is likely to be bad for the body.

Herbs are usually taken medicinally as teas: the herb is simmered for a few minutes and then allowed to stand before being poured out. You may find that some smell delightful, while others smell or taste unpleasant to you: you will have to experiment according to your taste and what seems to work medicinally for you. Suitable teas for some of the problems of premenstrual tension (including feeling faint, depressed, irritable, and so on) are: fennel, winter savory, borage, sage. For bloatedness and sore breasts try: pennyroyal, motherwort, raspberry leaf, camomile, rosemary, valerian, horse-tail, parsley. (Comfrey was once considered to be good for premenstrual bloatedness, but it has now been found to be a health hazard in large quantities, so avoid it).

All of these should be available in dried form in good health food shops. We should, of course, have mentioned dandelion – well-known as a plant best avoided by those with weak bladders!

Before we go on to discuss other possible treatments for PMT, most of which can be obtained from your doctor, we should mention that a number of women have found that yoga or acupuncture are helpful for premenstrual problems. We discuss these briefly on pp.52, with reference to painful periods.

TAKING VITAMIN B6 (PYRIDOXINE)

Vitamin B6, as we mentioned earlier, is available without a prescription. Pyridoxine was found to be deficient in some women who had been taking the oral contraceptive pill for some time, and it is now marketed as a supplement to the pill ('Comploment', for example). More recently, doctors have discovered that it is a useful treatment for premenstrual problems too.

Pyridoxine, as we noted in the last chapter, works at the level of brain chemistry. Hormones – either your own, or those in the contraceptive Pill – can deplete levels of certain chemical substances which occur naturally in the brain (the brain amines), and are involved in mood changes. In a normal menstrual cycle (ie. in a woman who is not taking the Pill), levels of these amines go up again after menstruation, so the depletion is only temporary. In women on the Pill, however, the levels of brain amines may be reduced for much longer periods of time. It is thought that many symptoms of PMT, which can also occur in women on the Pill (such as depression and irritability) result from this decrease in brain amines.

Pyridoxine is useful for PMT, partly because it works in a high proportion of women (as many as 75 per cent in one London study and in about 60 per cent in our experience) and partly because it is relatively safe. We won't go so far as to say that it is completely safe if taken in large doses over long periods of time: no drug is completely safe. However, it does appear to have minimal side effects, and certainly the authors and the doctors at St Thomas's Hospital who prescribe it regularly have not come across any when it is taken in recommended doses. It is not recommended if you are pregnant or trying to become pregnant, simply because *any* drug taken in the early stages of pregnancy *may* be harmful to the foetus, and it is wiser to avoid all possible risk.

You do not need to see a doctor to obtain pyridoxine: it can be obtained from a chemist without prescription. The drawback to this is that it is relatively expensive (a few pence a tablet). Alternatively, you can ask your doctor to prescribe it for you (in which case you only have the cost of the prescription). S/he may not have heard of the research on pyridoxine and PMT, so you may have to explain that research (mainly done at St Thomas's hospital in London) has shown that pyridoxine is helpful in many instances of PMT (especially depression and bloatedness), and that you would like to try it.

You will need to start taking pyridoxine for at least three days before you would normally expect problems to start – usually 10-14 days before the period is due. Suitable doses have been worked out by the doctors studying pyridoxine in London, as follows:

(i) If your symptoms are relatively mild, start with one 20 milligram (mg.) tablet at breakfast, and another 20 mg tablet in the evening. Alternatively, you could take one 50 mg. tablet a day.
(ii) If your symptoms are more severe, and they do not respond adequately to the doses in (i), then start with two 20 mg. tablets at breakfast time, and two 20 mg. tablets again in the evening. Or take one 50 mg. tablet morning and evening.

If you are taking the doses in (i), ie. 20 mg. morning and evening, and you find that it works most of the time, but does not work so well for the day or two just before your period, then switch to the higher dose (ii) for these last couple of days. After the first day of the period, stop taking them until the next time around. At these doses, there should be no side-effects, and no risk to your health. Pyridoxine is particularly good at relieving irritability, lethargy, breast soreness, bloatedness, headaches, and skin conditions such as acne.

TREATMENTS FROM THE DOCTOR

Women who experience particularly distressing premenstrual changes may not find that the self-help treatments, which we have outlined so far, are sufficiently helpful. If the problems persist and/or are particularly severe, then you may wish to seek medical help.

Medical treatments vary according to the problems and changes which a woman experiences, and according to the beliefs of the individual doctor. We outline the major types of treatment which doctors give for premenstrual tension in this section. We omit further discussion of pyridoxine as we have already outlined this. Some doctors, however, may well prescribe pyridoxine for you in preference to anything else.

You may, of course, be referred to a specialist, as many general practitioners feel that menstrual problems require specialist knowledge. If you are referred, you may be asked for urine and blood samples to enable the doctor to ascertain whether you are low in any hormones (such as progesterone). If you appear to have an unusual hormone output on the basis of these chemical tests, then the doctor may prescribe a treatment designed to correct this.

Whatever tests the doctor may carry out, it is in your interests that you understand the nature of the tests, and their results. If no explanation is given to you by the doctor, then you should ask her/him to explain the rationale for the treatment. Remember that it is your right to know what you are doing to your body.

Medical treatments which might be given for premenstrual distress include progestins, the contraceptive pill, diuretic drugs, and anti-prolactin drugs, as well as drugs such as tranquillisers. We will deal with each of these in turn.

Progestins

As we indicated in the last chapter, progesterone levels may be low in some women suffering from severe premenstrual distress. In this case, the doctor may advise a woman to take a progestin to correct the low levels of natural progesterone. There are some problems with taking the natural hormone, progesterone, as it is not soluble in water. Drugs which are to be taken as pills have to be soluble in water, so that they dissolve in the stomach and can be absorbed into the body. Pure progesterone therefore has to be given as injection or suppository, which has some disadvantages. The injections would have to be given daily at the time the woman would normally experience premenstrual problems. Since the hormone has to be given in oil, this can be quite painful. Secondly, pessaries and suppositories are rather messy and many women find them unpleasant.

As an alternative to progesterone itself, there are synthetic progestins: that is, synthetic hormones having a similar action to natural progesterone. Dr Dalton, however, who pioneered the research into progesterone and PMT, does not consider synthetic progestins to be as effective as the natural hormone for PMT. On the other hand, since the synthetic hormones are easily taken in pill form, many women might prefer to try them first. The commonest of these is *didrogesterone,* which is usually given in doses of about 20-30 mg. daily for about ten days prior to a period. This drug seems to relieve water retention in some women, and to a lesser extent, it can relieve mood changes. However, its usefulness in treating PMT is still under discussion in the pages of medical journals. Furthermore, since all progestins are steroid hormones, we do have some reservations about their *continued* use by otherwise healthy people: there has not been enough research yet to determine whether long-term use of steroids might harm your health. We must emphasise, then, that we have reservations about their use – through every cycle over many years. These hormones can be of considerable benefit in relieving distressing symptoms in the short-term, such as for short-term use in the menopause. Women who take hormones for PMT, for say, a few months, may well find that their problems are improved for some time, even after they have discontinued the drugs.

There will be a few women whose premenstrual distress is considerable, and for whom progestins provide welcome relief which milder treatments do not give. If such women discontinue the drug, their symptoms will return in their full severity. These women will be faced with a choice: either they take the drug, knowing that they may have to take it for some time, or they stop taking it, and face the symptoms. It may not be an easy choice, but we must stress again that it should be the woman's choice. If you are unhappy about taking hormones, then say so to your doctor, and discuss alternatives with her/him.

The Contraceptive Pill

Many women find that their symptoms of PMT are relieved by taking the Pill: others find that their problems get worse. Much depends on what type of Pill you are taking. If yours makes you feel worse, and you want to use the Pill rather than any other form of contraceptive, then you should ask your doctor for a different brand.

The medical profession, as well as many women, are now becoming more cautious about the Pill, especially since reports of its dangers to women over thirty-five, and to women who smoke. It is indeed true that although the Pill brought untold blessings, it does entail a risk to women's health. It is not a very great risk, but it is still a risk. We do not wish to go into all the hazards attached to Pill-use here, as there are many books dealing with it. We should, however, point out that using the Pill for some years may temporarily disrupt your own hormone production, as many women observe when they do not have periods for some months or even years after they have stopped taking the Pill. One consequence of this long-term disruption *may* be that you suffer more from PMT after you come off the Pill than you did before. There is certainly no evidence to suggest that the Pill makes your problems better *when you are no longer taking it.* It is only while you are taking it that PMT problems may be alleviated. Because of the health risks attached to long-term Pill use, we would not recommend women to take it *solely* for PMT. If a woman wishes to use it for contraception, however, it can be quite a useful way of dealing with premenstrual problems.

Diuretics

These are drugs which increase your output of urine. They operate by affecting the rate at which your kidney excretes minerals, and will usually be prescribed for premenstrual problems if these include bloating and breast soreness. (It is worth remembering here that pyridoxine also relieves these.) They may relieve some of the bloating by removing water. There are, however, some dangers attached to the use of diuretics: they can lower the blood pressure, sometimes dangerously, and can, if taken too much, cause the body's stores of potassium to be depleted. Having too little potassium can be dangerous, and can induce depression and weakness. These dangers are not very likely if you stick to the doses prescribed by the doctor, and if you only take the drug for a few days before your period is due, when the symptoms are at their worst. Under no circumstances should you take more of the drug than the recommended dose, even if you still feel somewhat bloated, as it may damage your kidneys if you overdo it.

But remember that there are easier ways of relieving bloating than taking drugs. The simplest thing to do, as mentioned earlier, is to restrict your intake of both fluid and salt (even in cooking) for a week or two before your period is due.

Anti-aldosterone drugs

These also have a diuretic action, as they make your body excrete more salt and hence more water. The usual anti-aldosterone drug which doctors prescribe is *spironolactone* (called 'Aldactone' when you buy it). Spironolactone does make you lose some of the water gained during the premenstrual period, and might be given to you in addition to another diuretic. It does not make your body lose potassium in the way that most diuretics do. However, like the aldosterone it antagonises, it is a steroid hormone. As we have said, we have some reservations about the extensive use of steroids by basically healthy people (we do not see PMT as an *illness* while we recognise that it can cause acute distress), and we certainly have reservations about the extensive use of drugs which affect kidney function unless they are absolutely necessary.

Nevertheless, if you and your doctor feel that anti-aldosterone drugs are what you should be taking, then the choice must be yours. If your doctor recommends that you take them, it is best to ask for an explanation. It may be that s/he has diagnosed that you need such a drug for some other condition, and that the PMT is in fact incidental.

Antiprolactin drugs

The drug which is commonly given to inhibit the hormone prolactin is called *bromocriptine.* Doctors are not completely sure how it works, but they believe that it acts in the same way as something which is normally produced by your brain, and which normally inhibits prolactin production. Women who are breast-feeding produce very little of this inhibitory substance, and so produce very high levels of prolactin, which in turn stimulates milk production. In some women, bromocriptine has relieved breast soreness, bloatedness and changes in mood during the premenstrual phase.

Bromocriptine is a powerful drug to take into a healthy body. On the other hand, your doctor may feel that the use of bromocriptine is advisable for a short time, especially if s/he has diagnosed that you have high levels of prolactin, as can sometimes happen in PMT. Bromocriptine is usually taken at a dose of 2.5 mg. daily. Larger doses than this can cause vomiting and nausea. It is most useful if your major problem is excessive bloating or breast tenderness, although it can help other problems too.

One other cautionary note: prolactin tends to inhibit ovulation, the release of the egg from the ovary. If you take a drug which inhibits prolactin, ovulation may become more likely. This means that while you are taking the drug, there is a slightly higher risk of becoming pregnant. So if you do have to take it, make sure that you use contraception unless you wish to become pregnant.

Danazol

Danazol is a drug which prevents ovulation and has been used successfully for the treatment of *endometriosis* (see p. 57). Recently it has been found to help some women with severe PMT and with breast tenderness. As its use for this has only recently come to light it is best obtained via a gynaecologist, or after seeking advice (see Getting Help, p. 67).

Drugs influencing the mind

Anti-depressant and tranquilliser drugs fall into this category. Anti-depressant drugs are really of little use for depression which only appears premenstrually, as they have to be taken for at least a week before they have any appreciable effect on your mood. However, if for some reason you are depressed anyway, you may well find that the depression gets worse premenstrually. If your depression is sufficiently severe, your doctor may consider that you should take anti-depressants for a while.

If your premenstrual distress consists predominantly of such things as anxiety, palpitations, tremor and so on, your doctor may suggest that you take a tranquilliser for the few days prior to your period. If you feel that the tranquillisers may help you, then it may be worth trying them for a short while. But remember that they make you feel rather dopey, and less able to cope with all the things you have to do: if the premenstrual phase is already a time when you feel that you are functioning less well than usual, then tranquillisers will only make it worse. More importantly, tranquillisers should only be seen as a temporary measure. It may be that you are suffering from acute anxiety premenstrually due to stress and strain in your life, which you only respond to when you are feeling a little below par. Perhaps you should think hard about the factors in your life which might contribute to that anxiety, and whether you can do anything to change them, before you start taking tranquillisers. Premenstrual tension means different things to different people. For those women with exceedingly severe changes, life premenstrually can be hell: an otherwise peaceful existence can be severely disrupted. For such women, pyridoxine, dietary changes, and all the other things which we suggested initially, may be insufficient. Drugs, of whatever nature, may be the only answer. Each of these categories of drugs has its advantages and disadvantages, as we have tried to indicate: we have placed them in the order in which we feel they are most useful.

For those women with less severe problems, however, women who are not virtually incapacitated with the premenstrual period, we would advise trying self-help methods first. Herbs or dietary change may be all that is needed, provided that you have the patience to develop treatments suitable for *your* body. If self-help fails, then you may have to seek medical help. But it is worth bearing in mind that self-help is based on the idea of developing health, of restoring the natural balances of the body.

The major problem with discussing premenstrual tension is that, though certain diseases may, in fact, become worse premenstrually (the incidence of certain illnesses is known to be greater in the week before menstruation), PMT is itself not an illness. It thus seems to us inappropriate to take drugs for it unless absolutely necessary. Many women are prescribed drugs for PMT when their symptoms are not, in fact, particularly severe, and they might be better off learning to cope with their changes, or learning to eat healthier foods.

5 Period pain: causes and cures

In our grandmothers' days, women were expected to put up with period pain, to bear it stoically. This is not necessary any longer. There are plenty of pain-killing drugs on the market for those who suffer considerable pain, and there are number of things which women themselves can do to help to alleviate the pain.

One in every two women suffers from some pain at menstruation. For most of us, the pain is not intolerable, and can be dealt with simply by taking an aspirin, or by massage, or other simple measures. It usually disappears within a couple of hours. We might ask why we have any pain at all: other animals, for example, do not seem to have any pain associated with their cycles, so why do we? It seems reasonable to suppose that in fact our bodies are not really adapted to having so many menstrual cycles – and it reacts accordingly. Biologically speaking, it is more 'natural' to be continually pregnant or breast-feeding, and it is that to which our bodies have become adapted in the five million years or so that human beings have existed on this earth. Women can now avoid having endless pregnancies, and so they have far more menstrual cycles than women have done for centuries. And perhaps it is because we are not biologically adapted to having all these cycles that we sometimes experience problems with them – such as pain.

For some women, menstruation is agony: with severe pain, which ebbs and flows like labour pains, and with nausea, fainting and dizziness. Doctors have tended to treat period pains in the past as an indication of 'weakness', even of neurosis. One gynaecology textbook, for instance, informs the reader that: 'Very little can be done for the patient who prefers to use menstrual symptoms as a monthly refuge from responsibility and effort.' It must be extremely galling, if you are a woman who does suffer from severe pain, to be told that you are using your periods as an excuse for not making an effort!

While there are undoubtedly some doctors who treat their patients as though they are malingering, most are now beginning to realise that women might actually *be* suffering. If you have bad period pains, and your doctor tries to dismiss it by implying that you are neurotic (or some such term of disrespect), tell him/her that you dislike her/his behaviour, which you find most unhelpful in dealing with the pain. One of the authors of this book was told by a GP that all women are neurotic! We imagine that, if he believes that of *all* women, then he must believe that women with menstrual problems must be doubly neurotic. If your doctor is particularly unhelpful, then you can insist on seeing another doctor, or asking for referral to a gynaecologist. No woman should have to 'grin and bear it'.

It used to be thought (and not so long ago) that pain in labour and menstruation was inevitable, and part of woman's lot. Some people even believed that women deserved the pain and that the pain proved women's inherent inferiority and weakness. (The Bible indicates that 'in pain shall you labour', as a result of Eve's part in the downfall in the Garden of Eden. For a long time, it was held to be morally wrong to try and alleviate women's pain in labour for this very reason.) Women are not weak, and do not deserve, or have to, put up with the pain. If you suffer period pains, then you can do something about it. It is up to you whether you choose to take drugs to alleviate the pain, or whether you would prefer to try other means. Perhaps you will try several methods of pain relief before you find something which is suitable for you. Be prepared to experiment.

PRIMARY DYSMENORRHOEA

Primary dysmenorrhoea is the medical term for severe period pains which accompany every, or nearly every cycle from the time a woman starts her periods. It usually begins shortly after the periods have become established in her teens. A common response given to sufferers is: 'Don't worry, dear, you'll be all right when you've had a baby' – cold comfort indeed to a thirteen-year-old who may have one hundred cycles before her first pregnancy (if she wishes to become pregnant at all). And furthermore, a small number of women have found that their pains become *worse* after having a baby. The 'have-a-baby' solution is, after all, rather drastic!

Period pain results from strong contractions of the uterus wall, which is, obviously, muscular. Both oestrogens and progestins can influence the strength of these contractions, and some doctors have suggested that excessive pain results from an oestrogen-progesterone imbalance. However, the cause is more likely to be related to another type of hormone, which has been discovered quite recently. Various tissues of the body have been found to contain substances called *prostaglandins* which seem to have a variety of effects in different parts of the body, and the uterus is no exception. Within the uterus, scientists have discovered large quantities of one called prostaglandin $F_2\alpha$ ($PGF_2\alpha$), which makes the uterus contract more forcefully. This substance helps to make the uterus contract during labour. It is also likely that PGF $_2\alpha$ is involved in causing severe period pains, as well as the nausea and fainting which some women find accompanies these pains. The amount of prostaglandin $F_2\alpha$ in the uterus of women suffering bad period pains may be as much as seventeen times the amount found in the uterus of women who do not suffer pain. Unfortunately, we do not know enough about these substances as yet to know much about how they work in period pains, or what might be done about it. Interestingly, many women who get pains have found that a couple of aspirin are more effective than many other, stronger, pain-killers: aspirin is known to lower the amount of $PGF_2\alpha$ in the uterus.

What Can You Do to Help Yourself?

Exercises: Certain exercises can help a great deal – although the natural tendency is often to curl up in bed and feel sorry for yourself. Even though you may not immediately feel up to it, you could try the following exercises:

i) Lie on your back, and bring one leg up toward your chin, and leave the other resting on the floor or the bed. Grasp the leg you have brought up toward your chin with your arms to take the strain, and keep the position for a few minutes.
ii) Lie on your back, close to a wall, and prop your feet up against the wall so that they are higher than your head. Lie in that position for five to ten minutes.
iii) Go down on your elbows and knees, and stretch your head and arms out so that your elbows are on the ground in front of you with your head between your arms. This position has also helped some women who have had pain after intercourse just before their periods.
iv) More strenuous exercises can help, such as walking, running, swimming, or horse-riding. Remember that women who lead sedentary lives are more prone to disabling period pains. So if you get much pain, it might be a good idea to try to lead a more active life.

Meditation: Meditation and yoga exercises are helpful for some women. They work primarily because they encourage relaxation – rather like the relaxation exercises involved in natural childbirth. Try deep breathing, and consciously trying to sit or lie still, and relax all your muscles. Even if the pain does not go away, you may well find that it becomes more tolerable – partly because you are no longer trying to resist it.
Acupuncture: Acupuncture can be helpful too. Unfortunately, most acupuncturists are outside the National Health Service, so you will have to pay for their services. You may be lucky and find a GP who

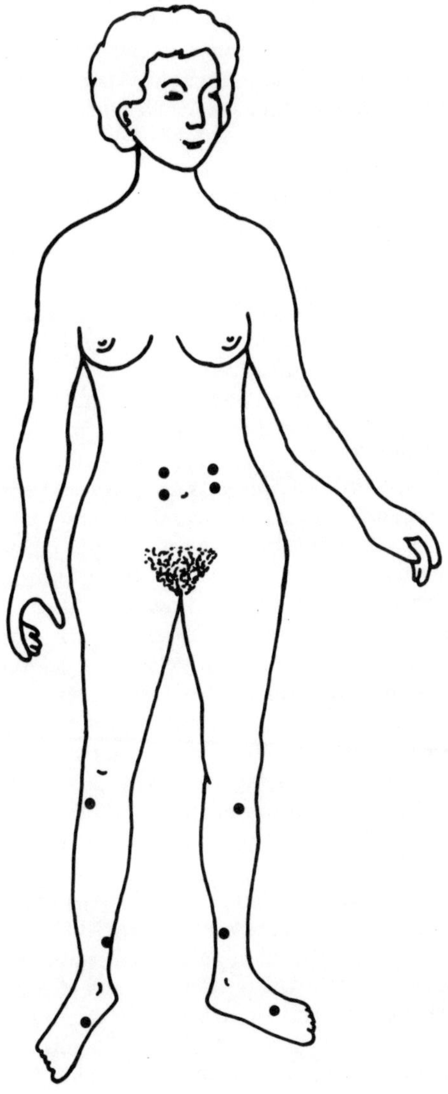

Figure 5: Acupuncture Points Known to Help in Menstrual Problems

Acupunture at these points (with acupuncture needles, or by massage) is known to help a variety of menstrual problems. Period pains are often relieved by acupuncture at the points near the knees.

practises acupuncture, but they are few and far between. If you cannot, and cannot afford to go privately, then you might try rubbing the relevant acupuncture points – a treatment known as 'G-Jo' in China (where acupuncture originated several centuries ago).

Acupuncture is based on the idea that there are several connected points on the surface of the body, which are linked to specific organs within the body. Thus, one of the points which is believed to help with period pains is on the knee, as indicated in Figure 5. The acupuncturist can insert a fine needle into these points which can then be turned slightly to affect the relevant organ. We understand from friends who have had acupuncture that the needling does not hurt at all. No one really knows how acupuncture works in pain relief – but it certainly does: indeed, the Chinese use acupuncture to obtain anaesthesia for major surgery!

If you want to try rubbing the acupuncture points indicated in Figure 5, rub them in a circular motion for about ten minutes with your thumb. It takes a long time before there is any appreciable effect, but if your thumb gets tired, you can always borrow a friend's!

Sex: A number of women have discovered that an orgasm is very good, as well as an enjoyable way of relieving period pains. It does not matter at all how you achieve the orgasm: masturbation is just as effective for pain relief as an orgasm achieved with a partner. An orgasm increases the blood-flow to the pelvic region, which seems to make the uterus relax, and to relieve the painful contractions.

The Pill: Painful periods often cease after a woman goes on the Pill, and may not return immediately after she comes off it. If you have tried other methods of pain relief and they do not work for you, then you might consider going on the Pill for a short time to try it out. Much depends on how you feel about taking the Pill for contraception, and for relieving a pain which you experience for only a few days each month.

Diet: Changing one's diet can also help period pains. One suggestion is to maintain a high protein/low sugar diet for the week prior to the period, as well as avoiding spicy foods and too much salt. For example, eat plenty of eggs, cheese, and vegetables, and cut down on the cakes, bread, potatoes and sweets. In particular, try to ensure that you have a high intake of vegetable protein, rather than protein from meat or fish: some people have claimed that vegetarians suffer less from period pains than do meat-eaters, which is worth bearing in mind.

Herbal teas (taken in moderation) might also be useful. We have found raspberry leaf to be good, but you might also try pennyroyal, fennel, and winter savory.

Calcium: Many women find that taking calcium supplements and/or eating more calcium-rich foods (eg. dairy foods) for the ten days before a period is due can lessen period pains considerably. Calcium can be bought in the form of *calcium lactate* from any chemist without a prescription. Alternatively, if you have a sympathetic doctor, you might ask her/him to prescribe calcium tablets for you.

Help From Your Doctor

If you see a doctor about your pains, then s/he might prescribe you a strong pain-killer, such as 'Paracetamol', in the first instance. Alternatively, you might be given a drug which counteracts the effects of the prostaglandins which are involved in the womb's contractions. The best results obtained with these drugs has been by taking them regularly three times a day for a couple of days before and for the first couple of days after the period begins. The commonest drugs of this type are *mefanimic acid* (eg. 'Ponstan'), which is taken at a dose of 500 mg. three times a day, and *flufenamic acid,* which is given at a dose of 125 mg. three times a day. Another drug which affects prostaglandin levels is indomethicin (e.g. 'Indocid') which is usually taken in a dose of 25 milligrams three times a day.

Don't worry if you cannot remember the names of these drugs; your doctor should know what they are, and will prescribe whatever s/he is familiar with. If your doctor does not know the research on prostaglandins, and about drugs which counteract them, then suggest that s/he looks at this book. Better still, take it with you when you consult your doctor.

These drugs do not seem to have any serious side effects, except mild diarrhoea or indigestion in a few women. Some people are allergic to them, and develop a rash. However, they are relatively new drugs, so we cannot be sure that they will *never* cause any serious side effects: we can only be sure that no serious effects have come to light so far. More importantly, their possible effects on the unborn baby are not yet known, so if you are someone who would not want to have an abortion if you accidentally became pregnant, then do not take them at all. It is best to take them only if you can be sure you are not pregnant.

A doctor might recommend more drastic treatment, such as surgery. This usually involves a D. and C. (standing for Dilation and Curettage – a scraping of the womb-lining, done under general anaesthesia). Any operation under full anaesthesia is a stress for your body, and you will be less fit for a while after it, so avoid surgery until you have tried other possibilities. It is not really known why a D. and C. works, but it does seem to help some women, at least for a while. Possibly it influences the production of prostaglandins by the uterus.

Occasionally, though rarely, pain with periods results from the womb being tipped slightly backwards (retroverted), which your doctor would discover on examination. If this is the case, then you can be fitted with a ring pessary, which fits over the neck of the womb, and which might relieve the pain. Alternatively, a retroverted womb can be corrected surgically if it is particularly troublesome.

Whatever course of action your doctor suggests, it should *always* be on the basis of a thorough examination. If s/he tries to give you something for period pains without having examined you, then you should insist on being examined, just in case you have something wrong with your womb. If you find this embarrassing, remind yourself that brief embarrassment is probably better than month after month of agonising pain.

SECONDARY DYSMENORRHOEA

Secondary dysmenorrhoea means period pains which occur for the first time in an adult woman. If you are in your twenties or thirties, for example, and you suddenly start getting severe pains, then there is often a specific cause. You should *always* see a doctor about it. S/he could then give you an internal examination, including a Pap (cervical) smear test. There are various causes of sudden severe pain in adult women.

Chronic Pelvic Infection

This is a chronic infection of the pelvic region (around the Fallopian tubes and uterus) which might have been contracted from sex, from an infection introduced by an IUD (coil) etc. It is associated with pain, which is often severe, in the region of the uterus. It does not only occur at menstruation, although it is often worse at this time, or after sex. It may be associated with a discharge from the vagina. The infection should be treated *immediately* with antibiotics – failure to do so can cause permanent damage to the Fallopian tubes and hence can cause sterility.

Fibroids

Fibroids are outgrowths of the muscles of the uterine wall, which grow like small balls on the inner surface of the womb. Fibroids can cause considerable pain, and are quite common in women over thirty. They are often associated with heavy periods. The only method of treatment is to have them removed surgically under general anaesthesia. In severe cases (which are quite rare), the gynaecologist may feel that it is best to remove the womb (a hysterectomy). If your gynaecologist suggests this, discuss the operation with her/him, and make sure that it is completely necessary: having such major surgery is not something to be taken lightly. A gynaecologist may only be prepared to carry out surgery if you are an older woman who has had children, and there are even one or two gynaecologists who seem to think that hysterectomy is a good idea for women who have had their children! If you are unfortunate enough to find a gynaecologist who glibly says that you don't need your womb any more, so it might just as well be removed, then find another doctor quickly. Only accept hysterectomy if it is absolutely necessary.

Endometriosis

This is a strange condition in which small fragments of the womb lining may grow in inappropriate places, such as in the ovaries, or in the abdominal cavity. As the hormone levels from the ovaries change, these fragments respond just as the normal womb lining does. Hence, they bleed when the womb bleeds. This is not in itself harmful, but it does contribute to severe pains. Endometriosis tends to occur more in women over thirty, and especially in those who have not had children. Treatment is taking hormones, such as those in the Pill, or occasionally surgery. The Pill, in fact, may give considerable relief from the pain of endometriosis, and many people who otherwise would feel unhappy about the Pill because of its unknown dangers have advocated its use for women with endometriosis.

Recently a new drug, Danazol, which works by blocking the production of hormones in the ovary has proved useful in the treatment of endometriosis. It has a number of unpleasant side effects, though, including bloating and sometimes nausea. Nonetheless, it might be worth considering it if your gynaecologist suggests it, as endometriosis can cause severe problems, which do seem to be relieved by Danazol. Sadly, there is no cure for endometriosis; the drug simply lessens the symptoms. If all else fails, your gynaecologist may suggest having your ovaries and womb removed. This is a drastic step – but only you know just how bad your pain is, and whether it is worth it to you to rid yourself of the pain.

I.U.D.'s (coils, loops)

Intrauterine devices (coils, loops etc.) often cause pain, especially when they are first fitted. (Incidentally, taking one of the antiprostaglandin drugs which we referred to on p.51 just before you have an IUD fitted can help to reduce the pain considerably. Ask your doctor about this if you are worried about pain.) If, however, you suddenly experience severe pain, particularly if you have had the device in for some time, then you must consult a doctor. It may mean that the device has slipped down into the cervical canal, and that the pains may indicate that the uterus is trying to reject the device. If so, it is useless as a contraceptive device – so get it checked.

Even normal periods can become more painful after an IUD has been fitted, especially in the first few cycles after fitting. Only you can decide whether the pains can be tolerated, and whether having an IUD is worth it for you in terms of contraception. If you are otherwise happy with your device, then you must find another way of coping with the period pains. It may, for example, be worth asking your doctor for a drug such as mefanimic acid (which is anti-prostaglandin) to minimise the pains of menstruation.

The message of this chapter, then, is that you do not have to put up with painful periods, as women had to in previous generations. If you don't want to take drugs, then there are a number of things which you can do to reduce the pain. If you feel happier to take drugs which completely numb the pain, then your doctor can give you these as s/he thinks fit. A very important conclusion of this chapter is that while primary dysmenorrhoea can be dealt with by yourself if necessary, secondary dysmenorrhoea in an adult woman usually means something is wrong with the uterus: so you should always consult your doctor. It may well be nothing serious, but it is foolish to try and forget it. It may not go away.

6 Irregular periods

HAVING NO PERIODS

Having no periods can be a blessing for some women, but for many it is a cause for anxiety. The commonest cause of having no periods is, of course, pregnancy. But if a woman knows that she is not pregnant, then she may well worry if she does not menstruate at all. Some women fear that having no periods may harm their health: this is not true – having no periods simply means that your womb has not built up its usual lining, so there is nothing to come away. This in turn may simply mean that you have not built up high enough hormone levels to bring about a build-up of the uterine wall. Not having periods will not harm your health, although occasionally it might indicate to your doctor that something else is wrong with your health.

There are many reasons for having no periods, most of which are quite straightforward. Next to pregnancy, the commonest cause is the Pill: many women experience a lack of periods (for which the technical word is *amenorrhoea*) for some months after they have stopped taking the Pill. While they will probably not become pregnant during this time, pregnancy is *not* impossible, and women who have post-Pill amenorrhoea should take other precautions. It may even be that it is a bad time to become pregnant, so soon after coming off the Pill, as your hormones have not returned to normal. This can take some months, or in a few cases, years. Post-pill amenorrhoea is not dangerous (other than the risk of pregnancy if you do not want it), but it is tiresome, since the normal sign of pregnancy is missing a period, and thus it is harder to know whether you are pregnant.

Primary Amenorrhoea

Primary amenorrhoea means never having had any periods at all. If a woman reaches the age of about eighteen, and has never had a period, then she should see a doctor. In many cases of primary amenorrhoea, there is a family history of later puberty and a late start to periods: in cases like this, it is highly likely that the woman concerned is also a late starter. If you have never had a period, then the first thing a doctor is likely to do is to ask you detailed questions about the women in your family, and their menstrual periods. If you intend seeing a doctor about primary amenorrhoea, it might be a good idea to check with your mother and sisters about their menstrual histories.

Another common cause of primary amenorrhoea is being underweight. A girl's first periods start only when she has reached a 'critical weight': this usually occurs just as her childhood spurt of growth begins to slow down, and she has reached a weight of approximately 48 kilograms. Similarly, if a woman's weight drops below about this weight, her periods may cease. In our society, in which it is fashionable to be too thin, trouble with irregular or non-existent periods is becoming more common.

Other, but very rare, causes of primary amenorrhoea are inherited conditions, and these often mean that the woman concerned will never menstruate. As these conditions (such as congenital absence of ovaries) are extremely rare, we will not go into them here. Such rare conditions would be determined by the doctor upon examination. Most instances of primary amenorrhoea can be treated – often just by gaining weight – so it is a good idea to consult a doctor if you are worried about being a 'late starter'.

Secondary Amenorrhoea

Secondary amenorrhoea means that your periods stop for more than about four months. Most doctors believe that treatment should not be given for at least six months, as, more often than not, the periods return on their own. Treatment based on drugs should *never* be given until you have had a pregnancy test to ascertain that you are not pregnant, as most drugs designed to bring on periods might harm the foetus.

Apart from pregnancy, being severely underweight is a likely cause of secondary amenorrhoea, and so is being severely overweight. People who are excessively over- or under-weight may have an upset hormone balance, which upsets the menstrual cycle. Another common cause of amenorrhoea is stress. If you change a job, someone close to you dies, if someone you know is involved in an accident – all these are considerably stressful, and can cause your periods to stop for a while. The only answer to shock-induced amenorrhoea is to wait until you have recovered from the shock: your periods will probably return eventually. If the stress continues, such as a stressful job, then you may have no periods or irregular periods for some time. Perhaps the best thing to do about this is to look carefully at the causes of your continuing stress: can you do anything about it, such as finding a new job, which would relieve the stress?

But what if you know that you are not pregnant, you are not too under- or overweight, and you do not feel that you are under undue stress, but still your periods don't return? We have mentioned post-Pill amenorrhoea, which can in some cases last over a year. Some drugs can also interfere with your menstrual cycle, as can some chronic diseases. For example, tuberculosis, anaemia and thyroid disease, eg. thyrotoxicosis, can both interfere with periods, and so can some anti-depressive drugs, so me major tranquillisers (eg. *chlorpromazine,* 'Largactil'), and some drugs given for high blood-pressure (hypertension). If you are in doubt about any drugs which you are on, and their effect on your menstruation, consult your doctor.

When you see the doctor, s/he should first of all take a full case history, and should also ensure that your weight is about normal for your height, and that you are not pregnant. S/he should also ensure that you do not have, or have not recently had, any chronic debilitating diseases, such as TB. This is especially important if you have recently changed your doctor, or if you are seeing a doctor associated with the Family Planning Association, who may not know your case-history. S/he should then ask you whether you have any other abnormal symptoms, such as milk discharge from your breasts (assuming that you have not recently had a baby), which might indicate that other things are wrong with your hormone system. Following that, you should be given a full gynaecological examination. The next step is to check on your body's hormone levels including ovarian, pituitary and thyroid hormones, in order to decide on the most appropriate treatment. It is imperative that your doctor goes through all these steps, as in a very small number of cases, amenorrhoea, especially if it is coupled with other unusual symptoms, *might* indicate something more serious, like a tumour.

In general, however, nearly all cases of secondary amenorrhoea are due to straightforward causes, such as having taken the Pill. Even if they require treatment, it is often very simple treatment, such as taking iron pills for anaemia. The best advice we can give, however, is that if your medical examination has shown nothing abnormal, you should wait. It is only if you are becoming desperate – perhaps because you want to become pregnant – that it is wise to take drugs. The best thing you can do for yourself in the meantime is to make sure that you are getting a nutritionally adequate diet. In particular, make sure that you are getting enough minerals and vitamins, especially iron.

If, however, you want to become pregnant, then you may wish to take drugs which induce you to ovulate. If your doctor has found that you do not have any anatomical or hormone abnormalities, then s/he might suggest a drug called *clomiphene* ('Clomid'). This works by stimulating the production of your own oestrogens. This in turn stimulates ovulation. Clomiphene is often used as a 'fertility drug', to enable women to become pregnant if they seem unable to otherwise.

The advantages of clomiphene are that it is relatively safe (ie. it causes few side-effects), and rarely causes multiple births. There is a *slight* increase in the frequency of twins and triplets born to mothers who have taken clomiphene in order to become pregnant For example, 8 out of 100 pregnancies resulting from clomiphene produce twins, while 1 in 90 of untreated pregnancies produce twins. Nevertheless, this rate is much lower than the multiple births produced by early 'fertility drugs' (these were a different kind of drug) – some of which produced quintuplets.

There are a few disadvantages to clomiphene, however, which is why we said that unless you are desperate to become pregnant, it might be best to wait. Firstly, you should never take it if there is any chance that you might already be pregnant, or if you have liver disease of any kind. Before prescribing clomiphene to a patient, a doctor should always carry out a pregnancy test. The reason for caution is that clomiphene can cause abnormalities in the babies of some laboratory animals, and it is not known for certain whether similar abnormalities might occur in humans – although doctors think that this is unlikely. The caution applies only to those women who might take clomiphene during pregnancy – the risk is negligible if you take it in order to become pregnant and you can be sure that you were not pregnant at the time of taking the drug. Clomiphene brings about ovulation *after* you have finished taking it, rather than during the time you are taking it. If you feel worried about possible effects on any child you might conceive, then maybe you should avoid intercourse until you have stopped taking the drug.

While no one can say for certain that clomiphene taken properly will not harm an unborn child, such cases are extremely rare. For women who are infertile for hormonal reasons, clomiphene holds out a promise of the longed-for pregnancy: few women in such circumstances would be concerned with such negligible risks.

The other slight disadvantage is that clomiphene may cause some side-effects in some women. These include blurring of vision, and enlargement of the ovaries, which can cause abdominal pain. They also include hot flushes, and nausea (as they stimulate oestrogen secretion). Of course, a woman who is anxious to become pregnant may put up with slight side-effects. Fortunately, such side-effects are rare: but if you are given clomiphene, either for infertility or for amenorrhoea, it is essential to notify your doctor if you suffer from abdominal pain, or if your vision becomes blurred.

Amenorrhoea with Milk Secretion

Yes, we know that having no periods and producing milk is perfectly normal after delivering a baby. It can, however, occur at other times, and may need medical treatment. It is due to an increase in the amount of the hormone *prolactin* which stimulates milk production, and suppresses ovulation. The most common reasons for this increase in prolactin with milk production (medically known as *galactorrhoea*) include certain drugs, or having just come off the Pill. The drugs involved are those known to increase levels of prolactin. For those familiar with drug names, or those who simply want to know, they include the *phenothiazines* (such as *chlorpromazine,* 'Largactil'), *imipramine, rauwolfia alkaloids, methyl dopa,* and *metaclopramide.*

If you experience amenorrhoea with milk secretion after coming off the Pill, then the best strategy is simply to wait, as the symptoms should soon subside. If they do not subside after a few weeks, then you should seek medical advice. If you experience these symptoms because of taking certain drugs, it may be necessary for you to change to a different drug, or a different dosage of the same drug: at any rate, you should see your doctor. S/he may consider that you should stay on the drug, and take something in addition which suppresses the milk production. Much depends on why you were given the drug in the first place.

In general, then, we would suggest that secondary amenorrhoea of short duration is best treated by leaving it alone, and making sure that you have a balanced diet. However, if you miss periods for longer than six months, or if you get amenorrhoea with milk secretion, then you should seek medical advice. Most women treat amenorrhoea with common sense: we usually know if we are not having periods because of stress, or because of being underweight – and we usually know when they have stopped 'for no apparent reason', which may need further investigation.

HAVING FREQUENT OR INFREQUENT PERIODS

Next to amenorrhoea, having too few or too many periods (that is, a cycle length much shorter or much longer than the average 28 days) can be a source of concern to women. Women expect their periods to be, roughly, every month, and become concerned if they deviate from that. In the first year after starting her periods, while her hormone system is becoming stabilised, a woman may not have periods every month. However, some women continue to have irregular and infrequent periods. This is not in itself dangerous, and need not be a cause for worry. Unfortunately, some women do worry about it, as they have been told that the average cycle length is 28 days, and feel that they are 'abnormal' if their cycle length is different. There is nothing abnormal about a cycle of 20 days, or about a cycle of 48 days: very few women actually have cycles of exactly 28 days in length.

The chief source of anxiety in women who have irregular periods, or infrequent periods, is that due to their irregularity they cannot always know immediately when they are pregnant. Such women should not believe that they are less fertile than other women: menstruation and ovulation are usually normal in irregular women. Ovulation tends to occur about 14 days before the period, even though the overall cycle length is much longer than 28 days. In other words, if for example, you have a cycle which is usually 35 days long (5 weeks), then three weeks usually elapse between the onset of your period and the time at which you ovulate: here your most fertile time is 21 days after the beginning of the last period. Those women who have moral objections to mechanical and chemical forms of contraception often have great problems with the rhythm method if they are irregular, or if they have a long cycle, and should try to follow their body rhythms more closely, using such methods as body temperature, and changes in vaginal mucus (which we described on p.16).

Medically speaking, irregularity is not a cause for concern, and it is not treated unless a doctor has reason to believe that the woman concerned is not fertile and she wishes to become pregnant. In such cases, she might be given clomiphene, as we described above.

Having 'too many' periods means that the cycle length is short – less than 23 days between one bleeding and the next. But by this we mean that the cycle is a regular one: if you have *irregular* bleeding at short intervals it may mean that something is wrong with your uterus. Irregular bleeding which starts in a woman who was previously regular should always be investigated by a doctor, as should any slight blood between periods coming for no apparent reason.

There are many causes of frequent, but regular, periods, some of which are associated with infertility, and some of which are not. If you are having frequent periods, you should consult your doctor in order to find out the cause. It will, however, help her/him in diagnosis if you know if and when you get a rise in body temperature (taken every morning before you get up). If your temperature does not rise (it is usually about one degree), then it may mean that you are not ovulating: if it does, then you are probably ovulating. If you get a temperature rise a few days after one period, but 14 days before the next is due, then it probably means that you just have an unusually short first phase (the phase from menstruation to ovulation in our Figure 2). If, on the other hand, you either do not have a temperature rise, or you have one which occurs a few days before the next period is due, then it may mean that your corpus luteum (which is left behind in the ovary after ovulation and which secretes the hormone progesterone) is inadequate, so that the fourth phase of your cycle is very short. This in itself does not cause problems, unless you are trying to become pregnant. Progesterone is essential for maintaining early pregnancy, so that if the corpus luteum does not survive for long enough, you are not very likely to maintain a pregnancy. Women with this problem (which is comparatively uncommon), can, however, be given progestins (synthetic hormones related to progesterone) shortly after ovulation in order to maintain a pregnancy.

We think that it is sensible for a woman who has *sudden* irregular bleeding, or who has very infrequent periods, to consult a doctor anyway, and have a full medical examination. It is unwise to leave these problems, just in case they accompany some serious condition which requires further investigation.

BLEEDING HEAVILY

At its worst, this may mean uterine haemorrhage, (bleeding from the uterus) which is a medical emergency. This is fortunately not a common occurrence, although heavy bleeding with each period may be quite common. Many women experience heavy bleeding if they have an IUD, for example, which will cease once they have had the device removed.

Some women routinely have heavy periods, requiring frequent changes of tampons or pads, while others have light periods which require little sanitary protection. Heavy periods as such are really only a major cause for concern if they start *suddenly* in a woman who previously had light periods. If this happens, it *may* mean that something is wrong with the uterus, such as polyps or fibroids, which require treatment. In fact, bleeding between periods (especially if you are not on the Pill) is more likely to indicate polyps or fibroids, than heavy periods *per se*. It can also indicate the early stages of cancer of the cervix – which can easily be treated if caught at this stage. It is thus imperative that any unusual bleeding is investigated immediately. Most women know the difference between what is normal menstrual bleeding for them, and other kinds of blood loss. Sudden heavy periods alternatively may be due to hormonal imbalances. If medical examination shows that you have a hormonal imbalance, and you wish to have the heavy bleeding treated, then you may be given a progestin during the second half of the cycle. If you don't like taking drugs, then there is not much you can do to lighten the bleeding, although you might be able to lessen the pain (see p.52). As before, a woman must be her own judge; whether she wishes to take drugs to lessen the bleeding or the pain, or whether she prefers not to, must be *her* choice.

In a very few cases, a doctor may recommend that a woman has a hysterectomy, if she has exceptionally heavy periods with considerable pain which does not seem to be lessened by any other treatments. Hysterectomy might also be suggested if the heavy bleeding is making a woman persistently anaemic. Although we think that too many hysterectomies are carried out in this country, often for no very good reasons, surgery for women with continual problems resulting from excessive bleeding and pain *may* sometimes be the only answer. Some women do benefit considerably from having hysterectomies for this purpose. Nevertheless, it is a drastic step, and you should be absolutely sure that there is no other answer for you before you decide on it.

Although heavy periods themselves may not worry a woman, they can sometimes cause problems. Not only do they mean worrying about changing tampons/pads at frequent intervals, but heavy periods can sometimes cause iron-deficiency anaemia. If you do have heavy periods, and you often feel tired, then you should try to make sure that you have enough iron in your diet. Iron is obtained from green vegetables, such as spinach, and meat such as liver. To ensure that you do not lose the important vitamins and minerals in cooking, do not boil your vegetables, but steam or saute them: this preserves the nutrients. You might also wish to take iron-containing tablets, which can be obtained from a chemist. But, as with all tablets, don't overdo it. One of the less desirable effects of iron-containing pills is constipation. So keep to the dose recommended on the bottle or by the pharmacist or doctor.

Apart from secondary amenorrhoea, which requires little in the way of treatment, this chapter has dealt mainly with conditions which require medical advice. While we have advocated 'home' remedies for some menstrual problems, such as herbal remedies for painful periods, this chapter has mentioned a few problems which are medically more serious. For these, a woman should always seek medical advice. Occasionally, women come across a doctor who tends to dismiss menstrual problems with 'It's just women's problems'. If this happens to you, complain. Menstrual problems *can* indicate something serious: your doctor should not dismiss them as trivial, especially if you have been sensible enough to seek her/his advice.

7 Tampons or Pads?

With so many products now on the market for sanitary protection, it is often difficult to know which is the 'best' one for your needs. Products differ in the materials of which they are made, their absorbency, and, of course, their cost. Each woman has to make her own choice of what seems to her the most suitable one for her periods, and for her lifestyle. Perhaps the most fundamental decision she has to make is between tampons and pads. Most women who are very active, including participating in sports, tend to use tampons, as they feel that they are less troublesome. Indeed, the manufacturers of most forms of tampons emphasise this in their advertisements; they tell us how we can carry out all our normal activities if we use their brand of tampon. Other women prefer to carry on using pads, particularly if they have very heavy periods, or are prone to vaginal infections such as thrush.

Until recently, most people thought that it was somehow more modern and up-to-date to use tampons rather than old-fashioned pads. Certainly, pads are messier and make you much more aware of having your period than do tampons. But recently, some rather nasty stories have hit the headlines about an extremely unpleasant disease which may be associated with using tampons, called Toxic Shock Syndrome, or TSS. Because of this, lots of women have stopped using tampons altogether. The trouble is that many of these stories get a bit exaggerated; after all, they do make good news for the papers. So how do we decide just *what* the risk is? Are tampons really as bad as all that? And are they *really* to blame?

WHAT IS TOXIC SHOCK SYNDROME?

TSS *can* occur in anyone. However, of the cases in America (where it was first reported) during the decade 1970 to 1980, 99 per cent were women, and of these, 98 per cent were menstruating. Clearly, TSS *is* associated with menstruation.

TSS is an illness involving high fever, headache, confusion, swelling, fainting, vomiting and diarrhoea. It is a very serious illness (which is why it hit the headlines) but, fortunately, despite the publicity given to it, TSS occurs very infrequently; for the years 1977 to 1979, for example, there were no more than 15 cases a month in the whole of the United States.

If it is associated with women who have periods, then what causes the disease? Doctors have investigated, but are still not entirely agreed about the cause. It seems that a tiny bacterium is involved. This *may* not cause any trouble, but if conditions are right, it is capable of producing a poison which gets into the blood. And it is this poison which causes TSS.

As we have said, no one yet knows exactly how this is associated with periods. But there have been some suggestions. A tampon soaked in blood at body temperature is quite a good place for bacteria to grow, especially if the tampon is left in for some time, and not changed. As the bacteria grow, they may produce tiny quantities of the poison. Using tampons does cause tiny irritations to the skin lining the vagina. Most of the time these cause no trouble at all, but *if* there are any infections around, it is possible for them to get into these little irritations set up by the tampons. So, the poison can get into the bloodstream and bring about the symptoms of TSS.

That is one possible way by which the bacteria may get into the body. But we have said that TSS is very rare, and millions of women use tampons every month without any trouble at all. So what happens to those few women who do get TSS? Why them, and not other women? We don't know the answer to that for sure. Some doctors have suggested that particular *kinds* of tampon might be involved, particularly the super-super absorbent kinds sold in the United States (but not sold in Britain), as these contain different materials from the less absorbent kinds. Another suggestion is that women are more likely to get TSS if they do not change their tampons regularly. The longer you leave it in, the longer it has to grow bacteria.

Whatever the theory, there are some practical points we could make. First, it is sensible not to leave a tampon in place for too long; it clearly *can* help bacteria to grow. Changing frequently is more hygienic. Another way of reducing the risk of infection is to use tampons for only part of the time, such as during the day, while using something else during the night. Second, it is wise to avoid scented tampons. These have been produced recently, and are sold with the promise that they help you to reduce vaginal smell. This is rubbish. The healthy vagina does not smell bad, even while menstruating. What does smell is *stale* blood. So if you remember to wash, and to change your pad or tampon quite frequently, then you should not smell. More importantly, scented tampons can cause more irritation to the sensitive skin lining the vagina.

There is, then, little need to be afraid of using tampons despite the stories about TSS. Millions of women use tampons without any trouble at all. The important things to remember are to use them sensibly, remembering to change them frequently, and to avoid using scented ones.

There are other reasons for preferring to use pads rather than tampons, though. First, you may prefer pads if you have very heavy periods, since they are generally more absorbent and it is easy to tell when they need changing. Second, you may prefer pads if you often suffer from vaginal infections, such as thrush. As we have indicated, using tampons may encourage the growth of minute organisms in the vagina, simply because the tampon remains at body heat – an ideal environment for growing germs! Women who suffer from persistent or repeated thrush infections tend to find that these infections flare up again at the time of their period as their body chemistry changes. If tampons are used, the irritation caused by the thrush can be made even worse, since the tampon tends to soak up the vagina's normal secretions as well as the blood. The vagina then becomes dry, which in turn makes it more sore.

A number of women who do suffer a lot from thrush have found that giving up using tampons can help to keep thrush at bay. It may seem inconvenient to give up tampons – but then, the inconvenience and irritation which thrush can cause may be even greater. If you do tend to get a lot of vaginal irritations, whether these are definitely caused by thrush or not, it might be worth considering giving up tampons. We do not know whether tampons might make other infections worse, such as *Trichomonas vaginalis* (or T.V. for short). This is a rather unpleasant infection which can cause a lot of irritation; it tends to produce a yellowish discharge, unlike the thick whitish one produced when you have thrush. It is certainly worth trying pads rather than tampons if you have *any* vaginal infection, though, since it gives the vagina a better chance to recover and to fight the infection.

An alternative to using tampons *or* pads is to use natural sponges from the sea. Many women have experimented with these and find them preferable for a number of reasons. First, the idea of using a sponge is that it can be re-used after it has been washed out and dried. As a result, you don't need many of them, so they work out far cheaper than any manufactured product. Second, they are very absorbent and can be used even if you have quite heavy periods. Third, they are very soft, and don't irritate the lining of the vagina to the same extent as ordinary tampons do.

If you want to try using sponges, you must buy a *natural sea sponge*; make sure you are not buying a plastic imitation sponge. When you have bought it, cut it into suitable size pieces, and boil them for a few minutes to sterilise them. If you want, you can attach a thread to them to make them easier to remove, much as a tampon has a string attached. The disadvantage of sponges for a lot of women is that they find it distasteful to wash out a bloody sponge, especially as this may sometimes have to be done in a public lavatory. Whether you choose to use them or not really depends on how you feel about this.

It has been said that sponges are not particularly hygienic, as they may have picked up chemicals from the sea, which you cannot completely wash out even if you boil them. This may be true to some extent – but it is also exaggerated. Most of the things which enter our vaginas are not sterile, and could all be called 'unhygienic'. Even tampons are not sterilised when you buy them. It's really a question of whether you would feel comfortable using sponges or not.

With all these things, the choice is yours. Your decision rests on the kind of life you lead, whether you are prone to infections, whether or not you find menstrual blood distasteful, and so on. It is very much a personal decision: we have considered it carefully here because of the widespread fears that TSS is caused by tampons.

Finally, it is worth remembering that whatever choices we make, we really don't have to 'grin and bear' painful and troublesome periods today. After all, as we said at the beginning of this book – why suffer?

BOOKS

Ann Kent Rush, *Getting Clear: Body Work for Women*, London, Wildwood House 1974.

Ann Kent Rush & Anica Vesel Mander, *Feminism as Therapy*, Random House Bookworkers Books 1977.

B. Kingston, *Lifting the Curse: self help for aches, pains, cramps and other monthly miseries*, London, Ebury Press 1980.

D. Llewelyn Jones, *Everywoman*, London, Faber 1978.

A. Phillips & J. Rakusen (eds.), *Our Bodies Ourselves*, Harmondsworth, Penguin 1978.

*B. Seaman, and G. Seaman, *Women and the Crisis in Sex Hormones*, Hassocks, Harvester Press 1978.

*P. Shuttle and P. Redgrove, *The Wise Wound: Menstruation and Everywoman*, London, Victor Gollancz 1978.

P. Weideger, *Female Cycles*, London, The Women's Press 1978.

Some of these are practical guides to keeping healthy and looking after our bodies (such as *Our Bodies Ourselves*). Some are specifically about the menstrual cycle and gynaecology generally (such as *Female Cycles*). Two are more theoretical but cover issues related to the theme of this book: these are marked with an asterisk(*).

Two other books which some readers may find helpful on some aspects of PMT are:

Judy Lever, M. G. Brush and Brian Haynes, *PMT, The Unrecognised Illness*, London, Melbourne House, 1979.

K. Dalton, *Once a Month: the premenstrual syndrome, its causes and consequences*, Fontana, 1979.

(We should say, however, that we have some reservations about the interpretations offered in these books; for example, we do not consider PMT to be an illness.)

A list of books is also available from the British Pregnancy Advisory Service, which also has a library: address, 58, Petty France, London SW1.

GETTING HELP

You will often find that the best source of advice and help if you have period problems is other women. If you do not know of a women's health group in your area, then form one of your own. Your group can gain a lot by discussing problems related to menstruation, but don't forget that you can help each other by techniques such as massage. Some of the books referred to above, such as *Getting Clear,* describe techniques of massage which can be helpful for period pains, for example. You might discover some of your own as well.

Women's health groups have been formed in different parts of the country, usually in major cities such as Leeds, London, Liverpool, Manchester or Glasgow. If you want to find out if there is one in your area which you could contact, write to W.I.R.E.S., (Women's Information Referral and Enquiry Service. This newsletter is printed in different parts of the country, so check the address from A Woman's Place, 48 William IV Street, London WC2, tel: 836 6081.) They can put you in touch with your nearest group. Such groups have been very helpful to a number of women, and are definitely worth trying.

Even if you don't establish a group, it might be a good idea to discuss with friends the possibility of setting up a 'hot line', so that if any one of you feels like screaming with tension or anger, you can immediately contact a sympathetic friend and talk it out. Failing that, it might be a good idea to phone the *Samaritans* (the number will be in the phone book) and talk it out.

Those women with serious premenstrual problems will probably have to consult their doctor. Unfortunately, the PMT clinic at St Thomas's Hospital now takes very few new patients, as they have very little money to run the clinic: they will now only take the occasional patient, referred by her doctor. A few PMT clinics exist in other large hospitals. Advice on getting help can be obtained from your GP, the British Pregnancy Advisory Service (58 Petty France, London SW1), Women's Health Concern, (16 Seymour Street, London W1 5WB, 01-486 8653), or from local Family Planning Clinics. Ask your GP also about your nearest well-woman clinic.

Finally, if you do have problems which you would like to discuss, write to us, c/o 21 Devonshire Rd, Liverpool 8.

BREAST CANCER

Carolyn Faulder
A Guide to its Early Detection and Treatment

One woman in seventeen develops cancer of the breast some time in her life. This honest, positive and reassuring book is Everywoman's guide to one of the most intimidating health problems she could ever face. It stresses the importance of early detection of a cancer, of good communication between doctor and patient, explains how early treatment can effect a cure and reminds women that a lump or cyst is not necessarily a symptom of malignant cancer. For those facing or recovering from surgical treatment, the author offers advice on the problems of convalescence and readjustment, and answers the many questions that cause patients the greatest anxiety.

'Full of helpful good sense . . . Carolyn Faulder knows her subject well' — *Guardian*

Carolyn Faulder is a journalist and author of several books, including *Talking to Your Doctor* and *Treat Yourself to Sex.* She lives in London.

THE EXPERIENCE OF INFERTILITY

Naomi Pfeffer and Anne Woollett

Recognising infertility, and going through the investigations, is a physical and emotional strain which can diminish the most optimistic. As a topic it is more or less taboo, yet it affects about one in eight couples. This book, offering comprehensive guidance to the causes, tests, treatments and cures (including adoption procedures) is the first to focus entirely on the infertile person. The authors have interviewed women with a range of fertility problems. They discuss their feelings of pain, grief and anger, and how their emotional and sexual lives may be affected — generating a sense of isolation and failure. But this is a hopeful book too — offering precise information on help available, and sensitively suggesting that one can come to terms with infertility.

Naomi Pfeffer is a Sociology research student: **Anne Woollett** is a lecturer in Child Psychology: both live in London.

A Virago Paperback Original